Bairns An' Feels *by* Charles Barron

The Snob Cross Incident *by* Moira Burgess

Scottish
Arts Council

D1339293

JP

Acknowledgements

The Association for Scottish Literary Studies and Hodder Gibson gratefully acknowledge support from the Scottish Arts Council towards the publication of this title.

For performance rights please contact the relevant author (see below) c/o Hodder Gibson, 2a Christie Street, Paisley, PA1 1NB, tel: +44 (0) 141 848 1606, fax: +44 (0) 141 889 6315, email: hoddergibson@hodder.co.uk

The Publishers would like to thank the following for permission to reproduce copyright material: **Photo credits** page 7 and 29–31 © Photodisc; page 8 © Alan Dimmick; page 33 and 69–70 © Photodisc; page 34 © Jonathan Alexander: page 71 and 96–88 © Nick Belton/istockphoto.com; page 72 © Andy Walters Photography; page 99 and 119–120 © Photodisc; page 121 and 146–148 © Famke Backx/istockphoto.com; page 149 and 171–173 © David Carrick/istockphoto.com, page 150 © Hodder Gibson.

Acknowledgements
BE-BOP-A-LULA Words and Music by GENE VINCENT and TEX DAVIS – © 1956 (Renewed) SONY/ATV SONGS, LLC – All Rights for the World Outside of North America Controlled by UNICHAPPELL MUSIC, INC. – All Rights Reserved – Lyric reproduced by kind permission of CARLIN MUSIC CORP London NW1 8BD

Every effort has been made to trace all copyright holders, but if any have been inadvertently overlooked the Publishers will be pleased to make the necessary arrangements at the first opportunity.

Although every effort has been made to ensure that website addresses are correct at time of going to press, Hodder Gibson cannot be held responsible for the content of any website mentioned in this book. It is sometimes possible to find a relocated web page by typing in the address of the home page for a website in the URL window of your browser.

Hodder Headline's policy is to use papers that are natural, renewable and recyclable products and made from wood grown in sustainable forests. The logging and manufacturing processes are expected to conform to the environmental regulations of the country of origin.

Orders: please contact Bookpoint Ltd, 130 Milton Park, Abingdon, Oxon OX14 4SB. Telephone: (44) 01235 827720. Fax: (44) 01235 400454. Lines are open 9.00 – 5.00, Monday to Saturday, with a 24-hour message answering service. Visit our website at www.hoddergibson.co.uk. Hodder Gibson can be contacted direct on: Tel: 0141 848 1609; Fax: 0141 889 6315; email: hoddergibson@hodder.co.uk

© 2007 Anne Donovan (Hieroglyphics), Janet Paisley (Silver Bullet), Alison Clark (Between the Lines), Iain Mills (In Love), Charles Barron (Bairns An' Feels), Moira Burgess (The Snob Cross Incident)
First published in 2007 by
Hodder Gibson, an imprint of Hodder Education,
a member of the Hodder Headline Group, An Hachette Livre UK Company,
2a Christie Street
Paisley PA1 1NB

Impression number	5	4	3	2	1
Year	2011	2010	2009	2008	2007

Cover photo © Ashley Coombes/EpicScotland.com
Typeset in ITC Stone Serif 10.5pt by DC Graphic Design Limited, Swanley, Kent.
Printed in Great Britain by CPI Antony Rowe.

A catalogue record for this title is available from the British Library
ISBN-13: 978 0340 946 282

CONTENTS

Preface

The Association for Scottish Literary Studies aims to promote the study, teaching and writing of Scottish literature, and to further the study of the languages of Scotland.

To these ends, the ASLS publishes works of Scottish literature; literary criticism and in-depth reviews of Scottish books in *Scottish Studies Review*; short articles, features and news in *ScotLit*; and scholarly studies of language in *Scottish Language*. It also publishes *New Writing Scotland*, an annual anthology of new poetry, drama and short fiction, in Scots, English and Gaelic. ASLS also produces a range of teaching materials covering Scottish language and literature for use in schools.

Enquiries should be sent to:

ASLS, Department of Scottish Literature, 7 University Gardens, University of Glasgow, Glasgow G12 8QH. Telephone/fax +44 (0)141 330 5309, e-mail **office@asls.org.uk** or visit our website at **www.asls.org.uk**.

This volume of plays was initiated by the Education Committee of ASLS. We are very grateful for the willing and fruitful partnership with Hodder Gibson.

Introduction

This collection of plays by Scottish authors demonstrates the wealth and diversity of writing being produced by those living and working in Scotland today. It should be welcomed and celebrated for that reason alone. If the Scots do not shout about their own creative output who shall? The Germans? The French? The Italians? All nations bang a drum – quite rightly – for their own sons' and daughters' work. The Scots, though, feel in some ways reluctant to do so in the field of the arts. If it were a football field we would be baying from the rooftops – or should that be the stands?

There are many reasons for this, not least of all insecurity about our national identity, a resistance to associate ourselves with the new in the event that we will be shown to have been wrong and misjudged our critical appraisal of a particular artist. I would answer this very easily: let posterity deal with all of it. Let it judge what joins the pantheon of great works that the Scots have been producing for over a thousand years. Let us celebrate that we still have writers in Scotland who are dealing with themes and issues that have a relevance far outside their homeland.

The great American author William Faulkner once said that if a writer writes true of one man then he writes true of all men. All of the plays contained in this volume speak truly. I believe that truth will find resonance wherever and whenever the plays are read or performed.

Although all of the plays are very different thematically and in the issues they deal with, they do all contain a common link: young people. I would hope that the young people who read the plays find some sense of recognition with some of the characters. I would also hope that the adult issues find an open mind and an understanding of human behaviour. None of the works here pander to a young audience and as a result do not patronise that audience.

Before each play the writer tells us something of themselves and their work. Although separate from each play this is a welcome addition and will hopefully increase the enjoyment and, in some instances, the understanding of the writer's craft or 'sullen art'.

Roy McGregor

About Liz Niven

Liz Niven is a poet and freelance writer who regularly delivers creative writing workshops to adults and to young people.

She has published four poetry collections including *Burning Whins* (Luath Press) and *Stravaigin* (Canongate and Luath Press) and is anthologised in Modern Scottish Women Poets (Canongate).

A former teacher of English and Learning Support, she has held residencies for a wide range of Arts bodies including the Scottish Poetry Library, Live Literature Scotland and London Poetry Society. She has been a Cultural Co-ordinator for creative writing in schools in south west Scotland and Scots Language Development Officer for Dumfries & Galloway schools.

She has written and co-edited many award-winning resources for educational publications, including *The Kist/A Chiste*, published by Learning + Teaching Scotland, *Turnstones 1*, published by Hodder Education, *Haud Yer Tongue* for Channel 4 and the *Scots Language in Education in Scotland* for the European Bureau of Lesser Used Languages. She is a joint setter for SQA for Advanced Higher Language Study.

See www.lizniven.com for further information or contact her publishers at www.luath.co.uk

About Roy McGregor

Roy McGregor was born and educated in Glasgow. He has written numerous poems, plays, screenplays and short stories. His short story *This is the End* will be published by Black and White in an anthology of short stories and poetry at the end of 2007. He has also been a reader for Hodder Gibson, who published his collection of plays for young people, *Dramascripts 11–14*, in 2005. He is currently working on his second novel.

Introduction to Activities

The Activities (written by Julie Laing) are aimed at pupils in S3–S5 studying courses such as Standard Grade, Intermediate and Higher English and freestanding Communication and Literature units. The work will be suitable for students hoping to achieve a qualification at Intermediate 2 level, or starting to work at Higher. References to the detail of specific courses and units has been avoided so tasks can be used with a wide range of classes.

Qualification differentiation arises from differing levels of support in introducing the tasks in the classroom and expectations of the quality of response. Broadly, in reading, practice in understanding, analysis and evaluation is given; in writing, opportunities for both expressive and functional writing are provided. Talk can be practised and assessed during specific talk tasks or through observation of pupils collaborating during research and discussion. A formative approach underlies, with opportunities for feedback and self-evaluation given; pupils are encouraged to assess their performance by applying the assessment criteria for their course (published on the SQA website). Extended critical analysis is tackled by asking pupils to produce mini-essays, which can then be used to write a complete essay if necessary.

About Julie Laing
Julie Laing has been a teacher of English, Communication and Media Studies for 17 years in secondary schools and further education and is currently a Lecturer in Media and Communication at Clydebank College. During her four years working in qualifications development at SQA she was involved in the implementation of National Qualifications in Media Studies and Higher National Qualifications in Communication and Media and remains a SQA marker and vetter for Media Studies. She was part of WW Publications which developed and published English coursework in the early days of Higher Still and has produced educational materials for Scottish Opera and Glasgow City Council.

Introductory research
In Scotland today, many varied and interesting languages and dialects are used, by both native speakers and learners. The writers of the plays featured in this collection believe strongly that texts in Scottish languages and dialects are as worthy of study as any others. You will enjoy these plays even more if you spend a little time researching the history and contexts of the dialogue.

Your research can contribute to your coursework assessments in talk and writing. The study of dialect and language forms can offer an alternative to the study of a literary text in the Intermediate and Higher course exams.

Activities

Give a presentation or produce an information leaflet/poster/booklet for your class about Scottish languages and dialects.

You could research areas such as:

- the separate languages that are used in Scotland today
- definitions (language, dialect, accent, slang, Standard English)
- origin – the history of how different languages were brought to Scotland
- how a dialect differs from a language
- attitudes to dialect use today
- the impact of modern trends (technology, immigration, politics) on Scottish languages and dialects
- whether Scots, Doric etc. are languages or dialects – academics can't agree on this so expect some debate
- current usage and status
- examples of interesting similarities and differences.

Give and receive feedback* from a partner on your presentation/writing. *Two stars (positive comments) and a wish (suggestion for improvement).

Useful sources

- Search engines (for example, in Google search box type 'define: Doric' for a range of definitions).
- Websites (for example, university/college language departments; societies/groups with and interest in the area (such as Burns societies)).
- Local libraries.
- Interviews: radio/TV documentaries; dialect/language speakers you know.

Research tips

★ Share research tasks and findings with others.

★ Keep a note of the location of all useful sources.

★ Don't follow up every link or you'll be overwhelmed with information.

Hieroglyphics

by
Anne Donovan

Anne Donovan

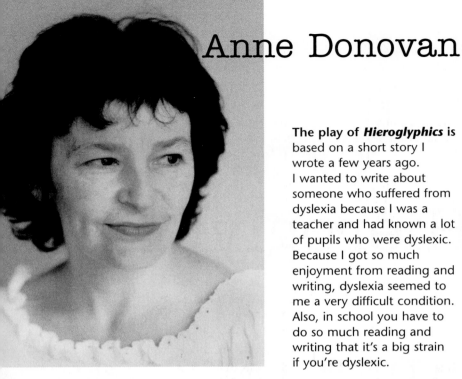

The play of *Hieroglyphics* is based on a short story I wrote a few years ago. I wanted to write about someone who suffered from dyslexia because I was a teacher and had known a lot of pupils who were dyslexic. Because I got so much enjoyment from reading and writing, dyslexia seemed to me a very difficult condition. Also, in school you have to do so much reading and writing that it's a big strain if you're dyslexic.

My approach to the story was to think myself into the character's mind. I've never had a problem with reading but I find it hard to remember strings of numbers. I tried to imagine how difficult it might be if the letters which make up words were numbers. I thought about the words on the page, imagined them jumping about and the first words of the story came into my mind:

'Ah mind they were birlin and dancin roond like big black spiders. Ah couldnae keep a haunle on them fur every time ah thoat ah'd captured them, tied them thegether in some kindy order, they jist kept on escapin.'

The story is in a Glasgow voice because that's the way the character speaks and it made it more real. I also felt that if you're dyslexic and come to school speaking Scots rather than standard English, then it's harder for you. In some ways the story and the play reflect an earlier time when dyslexia was less well recognised and there was less help available, but even with lots of support it's not easy.

The story was published in my short story collection (*Hieroglyphics and Other Stories*, Canongate 2001). I got the chance to make it into a drama in 2004 when the producer, David MacLennan, started lunchtime theatre in Glasgow at Oran Mor and asked me to do a play. By then I had published a novel as well as short stories but had only done two very short radio plays, never anything for the theatre.

Writing a play is very different from writing a story. Even though *Hieroglyphics* had a strong voice and character, the story would have to be told in a different way for the stage. I knew I had a very simple set and a maximum of three actors. That led to the play being written so that some characters could be doubled up. Also the play is basically set in school – first primary, then secondary – which involved minimal changes to the set. But for me the most important thing about the play and the story is the character of Mary. She is smart, funny, determined and finds her own way of communicating – I love her strength. In performance the same actor played Mary and Mammy and I think this reflects the way her loving family background helps to give her that strength.

Drama is a much more collaborative process than writing a story. I was very lucky to have Gerda Stevenson as the director of the play. She is so experienced as an actor, director and writer herself that she picked up straight away on areas where my original script was weak or unclear or not working; we discussed issues in detail before rehearsals started and I made changes.

One aspect that needed attention was that Mr Kelly is seen purely through Mary's eyes in the story but in drama all the characters have to stand by themselves. Even though Mr Kelly is a humorous character and a lot of his speeches are exaggerated for comic effect, I had to think more clearly about showing some kind of reason for his hostility towards Mary. That's why I added the speeches where he talks about his own childhood, to give him some background.

The people who make the play come alive are of course the actors and again I was blessed with three superb professionals in Frances Thorburn, Sean Scanlan and Linda Duncan McLaughlin. They rehearsed with Gerda for two weeks before the play was staged and there were some more changes at that stage. I attended some of the rehearsals and it was wonderful to see the play come to life. It was even more wonderful to see the first performance at Oran Mor. It was a great honour for me and I'm very grateful to all those concerned in making it happen, and a special thanks to David MacLennan for giving a fiction writer her first shot at a real play.

Anne Donovan

First performance details:
Hieroglyphics was first performed at Oran Mor, Glasgow, on September 6th 2004.

Director: Gerda Stevenson

Producer: David MacLennan

Designer: Annette Gillies

Technician: Duncan Taylor

Cast
Mary/Mammy: Frances Thorburn

Miss Mackay/Sarah/Miss Niven: Linda Duncan McLaughlin

Mr Kelly: Sean Scanlan

About the author
Anne Donovan is the author of the novel *Buddha Da* and the short story collection *Hieroglyphics* (both Canongate). *Buddha* Da was short-listed for the 2003 Orange Prize and the Whitbread First Novel Award, nominated for the Dublin International IMPAC Award and won the Prince Maurice Award in 2004. Winner of the 1997 Macallan/Scotland on Sunday short story competition, Anne has also written for radio. She lives in Glasgow.

About the play
Please note that phrases such as 'would of' or 'should of' or 'could of' in this play (and many other written versions of Scottish plays) are more accurate representations of the sounds made when the speakers are using the phrases 'would've' or 'should've' or 'could've', which in turn are short for the fuller versions 'would have' or 'should have' or 'could have'. Those last versions are how they should be written in standard written English, just in case your teacher corrects you for writing 'would of' etc.!

Centre stage, towards the front, are two school desks and chairs facing the front but placed apart from one another. To one side of the stage is a roller board and teacher's desk and chair with a waste paper bin close by. MISS MACKAY is writing on the board.

MARY sits at one of the desks. She has plastic letters, the kind that help young children learn their letters. She is moving the letters round and placing them on a magnetic board, turning them upside down and sideways, as if trying to make sense of them.

MARY: They were birlin and dancin roond like big black spiders. Ah couldnae keep a haunle on them – every time ah thoat ah'd captured them, tied them thegither in some kindy order they jist kept on escapin.

MISS MACKAY looks over MARY'S shoulder.

MISS MACKAY: Just learn the rules pet. Just learn them off by heart.

MISS MACKAY returns to the board.

MARY: But they didnae follow oany rules that ah could make sense of.

MARY holds up the magnetic board, on which MARY is spelled.

MARY: *(Pointing)* M–A–R–Y. That's ma name. Merry. But that wus spelt different fae Merry Christmas you write in the cards you make oot a folded up bits a cardboard an yon glittery stuff that comes in wee tubes.

It wisnae ma fault, ah didnae mean tae drap the whole load ae it on the flerr.

MARY stands, dumping the board and letters on the stage.

MARY: But how come flerr isnae spelt the same as merry and sterr is different again and ma heid wis nippin wi coff an laff and though and bough, meanin a bit aff a tree. Ah thoat it wis Miss Mackay that wis aff her tree, right enough.

MISS MACKAY stands at the board with a pointer in her hand.
She waves the pointer as Mary stands to attention at the front of
the stage.

MARY: A pride of lions.

MARY AND MISS MACKAY: *(Together)* A gaggle of geese.

MISS MACKAY: A flock of sheep. A plague of locusts.

MARY: We hud tae learn aw they collective nouns aff by hert, chantin roond the class, lookin oot the high windaes at the grey bloacks a flats and the grey streets, and sometimes the sky wisnae grey, but maistly it wis.

And ah could of tellt you the collective noun for every bliddy animal in the world practically. It would of come in handy if Drumchapel ever got overrun wi lions. You could of lookt oot the windae at some big hairy orange beast devourin yer wee sister and turn to yer mammy and say: 'Look, Mammy, oor Catherine's been et by a pride of lions' and huv the comfort a knowin ye were usin the correct terminology. Never happened, but. No even a floacky sheep ever meandered doon Kinfauns Drive. Ah never seen any animals barrin Alsation dugs and scabby auld cats till the trip tae Calderpark Zoo in Primary Four. And it was in Primary Four that ma ma came up tae the school.

MARY transforms herself into her MAMMY with clothing e.g. a hat from her message bag and squares up to MISS MACKAY.

MAMMY: She's eight year auld and she cannae read nor write yet?

MISS MACKAY: She lacks concentration.

MAMMY: She's lazy, d'ye mean?

MISS MACKAY: No, I don't think she's lazy; there is a genuine difficulty here. *(Reading from a sheet of paper)* Chronological age 8.7...Reading age 6.2... Spelling age ...5.7...Verbal reasoning...

MAMMY: Well whit are yous gonnae dae aboot it?

MISS MACKAY: We could get her some extra help from Learning Support.

MAMMY changes back into MARY.

MARY: They were nice tae me at furst, but ah couldnae dae the hings she wis geein me and she began tae get a bit scunnered. Ah could never tell them aboot the letters diddlin aboot, and naebdy ever asked me whit it wis like. They just gied me tests. Naebdy ever asked me whit wis gaun oan in ma heid. So ah never tellt them. And efter a while the extra lessons stopped.

MARY puts away the letters and stands.

MARY: They were dead nice tae me at school but. Maisty the time the teacher gied me the colourin in tae dae. Then when ah wis in Primary seven ah got tae run aw the messages and helped oot wi the wee wans. Gettin their paints mixed and takin them tae the toilet and pittin oot the mulk fur them.

MISS MACKAY: You're so good with the younger children, Mary. I don't know what I'm going to do without my little assistant when you go to the High School.

Bell rings. MARY puts on something which indicates school uniform (sweatshirt? tie?) and a big backpack. MISS MACKAY changes into SARAH.

MARY: A big rid brick buildin bloackin oot the sky. Spiky railins wi green paint peelin aff them. Hard grey tarmac space in front wi weans loupin aw ower the place, playin chasies in the yerd, joukin aboot roond the teachers' motors. The big yins, sophisticated, hingin aboot the corner, huvin a fly puff afore the bell goes. And us, wee furst years, aw shiny an polished lookin in wur new uniforms, waitin for wur new teacher.

MARY sits at a pupil's desk. SARAH looks round to see if there is another desk then reluctantly sits next to MARY. Enter MR KELLY.

MR KELLY: Good morning, boys and girls.

MARY and SARAH: *(Together)* Good morning, Mr Kelly.

MR KELLY: *(To audience)* I said good morning boys and girls. *(Encourages audience to reply)* That's better.

I will be teaching you History this term. And there are three things I will not tolerate in this classroom. One is talking, the second is insolence, and the third is sloppy work. Is that clear?

MR KELLY looks around.

MR KELLY: Good. Then we shall get along very well. Begin by copying the class rules off the board into your jotter.

He places jotters on MARY and SARAH'S desks, then rolls up the board and points to a list of rules.

MR KELLY: Rule No 1: The classroom is a locus for the pursuit of knowledge and the instruction of young minds, not a centre of entertainment.

SARAH and MARY write in jotters, MARY extremely laboriously. MR KELLY walks around while he is dictating.

MR KELLY: To that end, pupils will raise their hand and receive permission before opening their mouths. Rule Number Two.

He looks over MARY'S shoulder. He lifts the jotter, examining it as if it was something very distasteful.

MR KELLY: And what's this supposed to be – hieroglyphics?

While MR KELLY studies MARY'S jotter, MARY addresses the audience.

MARY: Sarky bastard. Mr. Kelly. Skelly, we cried him though he wisnae actually skelly; he used tae squint at ye through wan eye as if he wis examinin ye through a microscope and had jist discovered some new strain a bacteria that could wipe oot the entire population a Glesga.

MR KELLY: Do you know what hieroglyphics are, Mary?

MARY: Aye sur. It's Egyptian writin.

MR KELLY: Yes, sir, not Aye, sir. *I* is the first person nominative, not that any of you will know what that means of course, since you no longer have the good fortune to be properly educated in the classical tradition. Maybe if you would learn to speak properly you could then write properly.

MARY: The class were aw sittin up like circus lions, wonderin whit the ringmaister wis gonnae dae next. Sometimes teachers launch intae a big long speech and ye don't huv tae dae oany work. Which is hunky dory as long as you urny the wan he'd lamped oanty.

MR KELLY: So, Mary, if hieroglyphics means Egyptian writing, why do you think I am referring to your script using that term?

MARY: Because you cannae – can't read it, Sir.

MR KELLY: Precisely Mary. And since the function of writing is to communicate, what point is there in writing something that is utterly unintelligible?

MARY does not answer.

MR KELLY: Well, Mary, I'm awaiting your answer.

MARY: But if you were an Egyptian you could read hieroglyphics, sur.

MR KELLY: Are you trying to be funny, girl?

MARY: No sur.

MR KELLY: I thought not. Well, Mary, since neither you nor I nor anyone in this room appears to hail from ancient Egypt, you are going to have to learn to write in a legible hand.

He turns away from MARY. SARAH deliberately moves her desk away from MARY'S.

MARY: In Skelly Kelly's class aw ye did wis write, write, write till yer erm felt like a big balloon.

MR KELLY: *(Walking as he dictates)* The staple product of ancient Egypt was grain. As well as grain crops, the Egyptians cultivated vegetables and kept bees.

MR KELLY looks over MARY'S shoulder.

MR KELLY: You'll have to take that home and copy it out again.

MARY: Ah ended up takin piles a stuff hame tae copy up every night. Ah couldnae get oot tae play for aw the hamework. But aw that stuff aboot Egypt was dead interestin really. It was just the way auld Kelly done it made it seem borin.

MR KELLY: The ancient Egyptians believed in an afterworld. They built elaborate tombs – does anyone know what they were called?

MARY and SARAH raise their hands.

MR KELLY: Yes, Sarah.

SARAH: Pyramids, sir.

MR KELLY: Correct. Inside they were buried with artefacts that they believed they might need in their next life, for example, cooking utensils and even jewellery.

MARY: How did they know whit it wis gonnae be like?

MR KELLY: If you have a question, Mary, please raise your hand.

MARY: *(Raising her hand)* How did they know whit it was gonnae be like, sur? Ah mean, if you go tae Ayr fur the day, you could be runnin aboot on the beach in yer shorts or sittin in the cafe wearin five jumpers, watchin the rain pour doon. And if ye cannae prepare yersel fur a day at the seaside how the hell ur ye gonnae dae it fur yer next life?

MR KELLY: An interesting, if somewhat unorthodox, perspective on the epistemological philosophy of the ancient world, Mary. However, I would prefer if you would confine your observations to the strictly pertinent.

In order to safeguard their bodies for their journey into the next world, the Egyptians used preservative ointments and wrappings. The preserved bodies were called...?

MARY and SARAH raise their hands. MR KELLY indicates that SARAH should answer.

SARAH: Mummies, sir.

MR KELLY: Precisely. And on that note, do not forget to remind your mummies – and daddies – about the Parent's Evening. I look forward to meeting them.

The bell rings.

MR KELLY: Pack up.

MARY changes into her MAMMY. MR KELLY sits at the teacher's desk, first placing another chair opposite him. MAMMY enters waving a report card.

MAMMY: Right, Mr Kelly. Ah want a word wi you aboot this report.

MR KELLY: Certainly Mrs...?

MAMMY: Ryan.

MR KELLY: Mary's mother? Please sit down.

MAMMY: *(Reading from report)* 'Mary is functionally illiterate. It is a pity that the educational system will not allow such pupils to leave school and fulfill some useful purpose in society.' Whit's that supposed tae mean?

MR KELLY: Exactly what it says. Surely, Mrs Ryan, this should be of no surprise to you.

MAMMY: Well ah know she's crap at readin and writin. Always has been.

MR KELLY: That is a more colourful version of my comment, certainly.

MAMMY: But ah thought she was supposed tae be gettin extra lessons.

MR KELLY: Which, clearly, have not been too successful.

MAMMY: So whit are yous gonnae dae aboot it?

MAMMY changes back to MARY, and sits at her desk.

MARY: And the next day, the remmy wumman arrived.

Enter MISS NIVEN.

MR KELLY: Good morning, Miss Niven. Today we will be studying the history of Ancient Egypt.

MISS NIVEN: Great. I love ancient Egypt.

MR KELLY: Just as well, Miss Niven, since we have an expert here. Mary Ryan. Would you like to take your little charge away somewhere, Miss Niven? She's a poor soul, but seems harmless. Tries.

MARY: Obviously, no bein able tae read makes you deif.

MISS NIVEN: As you know, Mr Kelly, I'm here to support all the pupils.

MR KELLY: Now, Miss Niven. I've been teaching for thirty-five years. Save that line for the policy documents. But if you'd rather stay, of course you're very welcome.

MISS NIVEN: Thank you, Mr Kelly.

MISS NIVEN draws a chair over and sits down beside MARY.

MR KELLY: The task of Egyptian religious practice lay predominantly in keeping the divine order and in defending life from the agents of chaos.

As MR KELLY lectures the class, MISS NIVEN helps MARY. Though she is speaking quietly her voice is audible as MR KELLY speaks.

MR KELLY: Miss Niven, is there a problem?

MISS NIVEN: Not at all Mr Kelly, just helping Mary with the spelling of some of these words.

MR KELLY: *(Quietly)* I demand silence in my classroom and I find that that my flow is a little hampered by your conversation, Miss Niven. I'd really prefer if you and Mary went elsewhere.

MISS NIVEN: I don't want Mary to miss History, Mr Kelly. It's important she has access to the whole curriculum.

MR KELLY: Your devotion to her education is admirable, but surely it's more important that she masters the basics – couldn't you take this child away somewhere and give her extra tuition in English or Maths.

MARY: But ah'm no remmy at maths.

MR KELLY: I beg your pardon?

MARY: Ah'm no remmy at maths – it's jist ah cannae read the stuff. If sumbdy tells me whit tae dae ah kin dae it, ah jist cannae read it masel in thae wee booklets.

MR KELLY: What are you talking about, girl?

MARY: See – the numbers never birl aroond the way the letters dae; mibbe its because there urny usually as many numbers in a number as there are letters in a word, d'you know whit ah mean? Or is it because ye read them across the way and ye dae maths doon the way? Mibby if ah lived in wanny thae countries where they wrote doon the way ah'd be aw right. Ah mean there's aw kinds a ways a writin in the world. Some folk read right tae left and some up and doon. And they Egyptians drew wee pictures fur their writin. Ah hink ah should of been an Egyptian.

MR KELLY: Witless. I rest my case.

MISS NIVEN: Mr Kelly, could we maybe have a discussion about your methodology – I don't feel it's entirely appropriate for...

MR KELLY: Pedagogy, Miss Niven, pedagogy.

MISS NIVEN: Look, suppose I go to the library and get some books on Ancient Egypt – they have some with beautiful illustrations.

MR KELLY: Yes, I believe they now have books suited to all ranges of ability.

Exit MISS NIVEN.

MR KELLY: Methodology – policy documents – all this twittering and wittering that goes on nowadays. Every child in the same classroom no matter what their ability. The teacher must cater for all pupils – cater for them, as if my job is to give them a choice of egg mayonnaise or ham sandwiches.

MARY: Sir, have we tae write this doon?

MR KELLY: It used to be so different. I taught Classics then.

MARY: He's away again.

MR KELLY: The beauty and rigour of Latin, the poetry of ancient Greek. Of course they removed it from the syllabus. Apparently, Classics is considered very elitist now.

MARY: Ah've started so ah'll finish.

MR KELLY: Elitist! My father was a labourer, my mother a machinist. But they took me to the library every Saturday, we listened to concerts on Radio 3. In those days working class didn't mean signing on the dole wearing a Burberry baseball cap. Education was the way out and up for children like me.

MARY: Noo the bit aboot the scholars.

MR KELLY: Of course we scholars were in a separate stream, not held back by those who were unable to benefit from academic study. But now the buzzword is social inclusion. The Head Teacher says the pupils need transferable skills.

Enter MISS NIVEN with a pile of library books on the Egyptians, which she places on MARY'S desk. Exit MISS NIVEN. MARY starts to look at the books.

MR KELLY: The man's an idiot – wouldn't know a transferable skill if it struck him on the back and rent his Armani suit into shreds. What does Classics teach if not transferable skills? Grammar, structure, composition, logic, appreciation of beauty. Some people can't recognise beauty, even when it's underneath their noses.

MR KELLY goes to his desk.

MARY: It's amazin – the way they Egyptians done their writin. Pictures insteidy letters. Nae worryin aboot whit kindy wood it wis or how many e's in tea. It must of been that easy compared tae writin words.

MR KELLY: Stop talking, Mary Ryan. I'm going to give you all out your tests that you did last week.

MR KELLY walks round giving out essays to the members of the audience near the front. There are a few red marks on them, brief comments.

MR KELLY: Not bad. Good work here. A big improvement.

He holds MARY'S up high. It is a mess and covered in red marks all over.

MR KELLY: Once again, Mary Ryan, I cannot read a word of your writing.

MARY: Ah cannae read a word of his writin either – but ah cannae say that, can ah?

MR KELLY places MARY'S work on her desk. She looks at it.

MARY: Looks as if it's bleedin.

Enter MISS NIVEN.

MISS NIVEN: Good morning Mr Kelly. Morning, boys and girls.

MR KELLY: A word, Miss Niven.

He picks up MARY'S test and shows it to MISS NIVEN.

MR KELLY: Look at this. Nought per cent. When are you going to do something about this child?

MISS NIVEN: When am I going to do something about her? You make her sound like a problem.

MR KELLY: If a child is getting no marks in a simple test about ancient Egyptian life and culture – God, the dreadful names they give these topics nowadays – if she gets zero per cent in spite of your ministrations then surely it's time for more concerted action.

MISS NIVEN: I couldn't agree more, Mr Kelly. So, when can we meet and draw up an action plan?

She produces big filofax.

MR KELLY: Action plan? Miss Niven, when are you going to take this poor child out of my classroom and teach her to read and write?

MISS NIVEN: It's not that simple.

MR KELLY: It seems very simple to me. If she cannot read and write then she cannot function in a normal classroom. And it's your job to take her away and drill her in the basics.

MISS NIVEN: Mr Kelly, my job is to ensure that she experiences the full range of the curriculum. If she's unable to access it in the traditional print medium, then it is my job to support you in facilitating alternative methodologies.

MR KELLY: For God's sake woman, would you stop talking gobbledygook? What are you going to do about this?

MISS NIVEN hands MARY a small recorder/player and indicates the controls to her.

MISS NIVEN: The red button is for record...

MR KELLY: Miss Niven, I'm aware Mary is no scholar, but I'm not having her listening to Radio Clyde instead of...

MISS NIVEN: Mr Kelly, you've made it impossible for me to offer any support in this classroom – you won't budge even an inch. The recorder is to allow Mary to tape your lessons and listen to them at home. Surely you can have no objection to that?

MR KELLY: The other pupils might think it is unfair that Mary does not have to do the writing.

MISS NIVEN: And since when have you ever cared about what pupils thought about anything?

MISS NIVEN and MR KELLY look at each other for a moment.

MISS NIVEN: *(To MARY)* I'll see you in English next period, okay?

EXIT MISS NIVEN. MISS NIVEN changes into SARAH.

MR KELLY: The early dynastic period – Dynasties One to Three – lasted from circa 3100 to 2613 BC.

MARY: So there ah was, stuck at ma desk, listenin tae Mr Kelly dronin on as usual.

MR KELLY: Writing now appeared in Egypt, shortly after it was invented in Sumer.

MARY: But ah didnae have tae write doon his notes any mair. That meant Miss Niven had solved his problem, ma problem and her ain problem so she pissed aff tae help some other poor wee soul.

MR KELLY: The ancient Egyptian language belongs to an Afro-Asiatic group including Berber, Chadic, Arabic and Hebrew.

MR KELLY writes these names on the board.

MARY: So ah sat and drew wee pictures insteidy words, like the Egyptians. At first ah copied the wans in the book, then ah started makin up ma ain. Turnt oot tae be dead good at it. Somehow the pictures seemed tae come intae ma heid and it wis that easy compared tae writin words. If ye wanted tae say 'would you like a cup of tea?' ye jist drew a wee cup'n'saucer and a mooth and a question mark. Nae worryin aboot whit kindy wood it wis or how many e's in tea. Ah spent ages gettin them jist right and colourin them in wi felties. And that was that, till the next parents' night.

MARY changes into MAMMY. MR KELLY sits at desk and places chair opposite.

MR KELLY: Good evening Mrs Ryan.

MAMMY: Right Mr Kelly. Ah want tae know whit's gaun oan in this school.

MR KELLY: We have something in common there, Mrs Ryan.

MAMMY: Mary's tellin me the remmy wumman's left and she's got this thing insteid.

Produces tape recorder from her bag and places it on MR KELLY'S desk.

MR KELLY: Indeed.

MAMMY: Look son, ah'm no meanin tae be cheeky or that, but ah'm sick of listenin tae your voice dronin on. Every night she's listenin tae these tapes, over and over. You'd think you were a boy band. Ah can hardly hear Eastenders for it.

MR KELLY: I'm very sorry to hear that.

MAMMY: It's okay, ah can catch the omnibus on a Sunday. Anyway, that's no the point. See, whit you have tae understaund is that Mary is actually dead conscientious. And she's no daft.

MR KELLY: I don't think anyone ever tried to insinuate...

MAMMY: So how come she's no gettin any better at school?

MR KELLY: I am unable to shed any light on the matter.

MAMMY: This is whit ah've been tryin tae get an answer tae for years...for years ah've been listenin tae teachers tellin me that they're gonnae try this, that and the next thing. She's dyslexic, she's got a learnin deficit, she's got special needs. Ma arse. And at the end of the day where are we? Where are we, Mr Kelly?

MR KELLY: I...

MAMMY: Ah'll tell you where, Mr Kelly, we're nae further forward.

MAMMY changes back into MARY. who sits down at her desk. SARAH sits at the other desk.

MR KELLY: I had a very interesting chat with your mother at the Parents' Night, Mary. She, like me, seems to think that the tape recorder is not a helpful option. *(He dumps the tape recorder in the bin)* I think you should return to the more traditional methods of communicating, namely paper and pen.

Sarah, would you move over here, please.

SARAH moves her desk next to next to MARY'S.

MR KELLY: You can copy Sarah's notes if you fall behind.

MARY: And Sarah was very willing tae help.

The bell rings.

MARY: Gonnae gies a lenny yer jotter tae copy up the day's notes?

SARAH: *(Loudly)* Of course, Mary.

MR KELLY: Thank you Sarah.

Exit MR KELLY, smiling.

SARAH: That'll be a pound.

MARY: Whit fur?

SARAH: Wan night's loan of ma jotter.

MARY: Aye, right.

SARAH: D'you want it or no?

MARY: Ah cannae afford tae gie you a pound every day.

SARAH: Suit yersel.

MARY: But the next day Skelly Kelly got intae the act.

Enter MR KELLY. He looks at MARY'S jotter.

MR KELLY: Where are your notes, Mary?

MARY shrugs.

MR KELLY: Don't try to be insolent with me, girl. I told you to get a copy from Sarah. Sarah, didn't you give your jotter to Mary yesterday?

SARAH: I offered it to her, sir, but she never took it home.

MR KELLY: What do you have to say for yourself?

MARY does not answer.

MR KELLY: This is intolerable. Everyone runs around, trying to help you. You sit there and do nothing, don't make the slightest effort to help yourself. Expect the world to revolve around you. Typical. I shall not waste another second on you. As far as I'm concerned you will do the work of the class like everyone else, with no concessions made to your so-called learning difficulties. And if you can't keep up, well so be it, young lady.

MARY: If you can't keep up, so be it. Whit the hell was he talkin aboot? It's like expectin a dunkey tae keep up wi a field a racehorses.

MR KELLY: *(Dictates notes in race commentator style)* In the twenty-fifth Dynasty, the calligraphic and shorthand branches of cursive writing diverged so far that they form two separate scripts known as hieratic and abnormal hieratic...

MARY: Ah was the wan that fell at the first fence.

MR KELLY: Abnormal hieratic is the shorthand used for administrative documents...

MARY: Ah just sat there, day after day, wi a pen in ma haund.

MR KELLY: The new standardised shorthand, which probably developed separately in Lower Egypt at the same time as the abnormal hieratic...

MARY: Ah couldnae understaund him. Whit was he tryin tae prove? He could of gied me chores tae dae, ah could of been useful – run his messages, cleaned the board. Nae chance.

MR KELLY: Was called demotic.

MARY: Then wan day, ah'd had enough.

MARY goes round the audience putting paper out on each table.

MR KELLY: Today you will be doing a timed composition. This is to give you practice for the so-called Imaginative Response to Historical Lifestyles question in the examination. A wishy-washy piece of nonsense, which, were I in charge of the syllabus, would disappear without trace, but, since that is not the case, we must needs get through it. The question is on the board. *(Rolls up board to indicate question)* 'The ancient Egyptians took objects with them to help them in their next lifetime. Imagine you are going on a journey to the next world. Describe where you are going and what things you would take with you.' You have fifty minutes. Begin.

MR KELLY sits at his desk, marking papers.

MARY: Ah sat for a minute and thought, tried tae imagine ma journey and the hings ah'd take wi me. And ah started ma essay, but insteidy writin, ah done it aw in wee pictures. Ah drew me and ma mammy (*ma da might as well be in the next world fur aw we see of him*) and ma sisters, Catherine an Elizabeth – in a boat, fur ah wanted ma journey tae be ower the watter. Ah spent a long time thinkin oot whit we'd take. Some of the hings we huv in this world might no be oany use tae us in the next. After aw, whit use are CDs if there's nae electricity? Ah decided tae gie each ae us three hings tae take in the boat fur three is wanny they numbers that's gey important in stories. Who ever heardy emdy gettin five wishes aff their fairy godmother? Elizabeth's were easy cause she's only four an she aye cairries a bitty auld blanket roond wi her, and she'd want her teddy and her dolly. Catherine's eight – she'd take her teddy and her new blue jumper and her deelie-boablers; ye know they hings ye pit roond yer heid wi antennaes stickin oot fae them an they make ye look lik sumpn fae ooter space. Some day she'll feel like a real chookie when she minds she wanted tae go tae mass in them, but just noo she'd want tae take them. And ah'd take some paper and the black pen fur daein ma wee pictures, and ma photie ae a wee spaniel pup that ah cut oot a magazine and keep on the wall by ma bed, fur we cannae huv a real dug doon ma bit. But whit would ma mammy take wi her? It'd need tae be sumpn private and jist fur her, and mammies don't tell ye these things fur they're too busy workin and bringin ye up.

MR KELLY: Finish the word you are on and put down your pen.

MARY: It wis time, and ah hud tae leave her wi nothin. But mibbe no. Bet if ah asked her, Mammy'd say we are her three best hings; Catherine and Elizabeth and me.

MR KELLY: Mary Ryan, collect in the compositions.

MARY walks round gathering in the papers.

MARY: Aw they different kinds a haundwritin; squinty, straight, big or wee, different sizes and shapes on the page. And here's ma story wi its neat wee black drawins – *(She shows audience)* – right on tap ae the pile.

MARY takes the pile of papers, and places it on MR KELLY'S desk. She stands beside the desk, waiting. MR KELLY looks at MARY'S paper, lifts it, looks at MARY.

MR KELLY: And what's this supposed to be?

MARY: *(Grinning at audience)* Hieroglyphics.

END OF PLAY

ACTIVITIES

Warm up – In Mary's Shoes

Describe to a partner, *without using or mouthing words*, your day so far.

Watch your partner's description.

Feedback to your group/class what you learned from this experience.

The rules

You have two minutes each to describe your day.

You can use a combination of: gestures, facial expression, mime, drawings.

Research – Dyslexia

Find out about dyslexia from a range of sources.

Organise your findings under headings (for example, diagnosis, where to get help…)

Write the copy for a leaflet or webpage about dyslexia.

Purpose – to raise awareness about dyslexia.

Audience – young people your age.

Aims – make it easier for young people to recognise the condition; show them where to get help and advice; counter negative attitudes.

Research tips

★ Sources: websites, Learning Support Department, libraries, relevant charities, interviews with/case-studies of people with dyslexia; Mary's (fictional) account of how she copes with the condition.

★ Don't follow up every website link as you will end up with too much information.

★ Other educational leaflets/websites aimed at your age group.

★ Share research tasks with others and share your findings.

★ Keep a note of the location of all useful sources in case you need to look at them again or refer to them in a bibliography.

Personal/reflective writing

MARY: Ah sat for a minute and thought, tried tae imagine ma journey and the hings ah'd take wi me.

1 Read the speech Mary makes before she hands in her essay to Mr Kelly.

List all the people Mary would take on the boat to the next lifetime.

List the items they would take with them. (You might not find three for each person.) Suggest what their choices tell you about them.

Example

Who	First item	Second item	Third item
Catherine	Teddy	New blue jumper	Deelie-boablers
What the item suggests about the person	A child, maybe needs comfort	Cares about what she wears	Likes a joke, doesn't take self too seriously

List the three items *you* would choose to take. (If you don't believe in a 'next lifetime', think about a very long journey.)

Make notes on what each item means to you and why you would want to take it.

2 This is the essay Mr Kelly asked Mary and her class to write.

The ancient Egyptians took objects with them to help them in their next lifetime. Imagine you are going on a journey to the next world. Describe where you are going and what things you would take with you.

Do Mr Kelly's essay as either a personal/reflective essay or a talk presentation.

Assess your work and the work of one other person using the criteria for writing/talking on the course you are doing.

Give your partner 'two stars and a wish' – two positive comments about their work and one suggestion on how to improve it.

Silver Bullet

by
Janet Paisley

CHARACTERS

ALEX, *father and radio storyteller*

MEG, *mother and radio guest speaker*

WATTIE, *son and radio presenter*

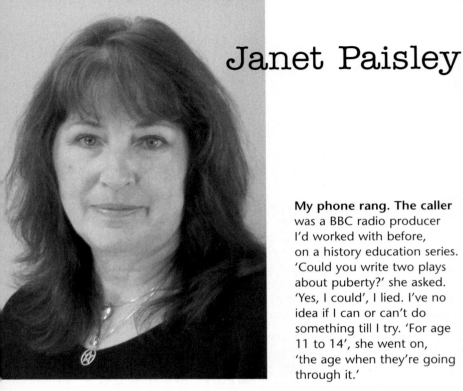

Janet Paisley

My phone rang. The caller was a BBC radio producer I'd worked with before, on a history education series. 'Could you write two plays about puberty?' she asked. 'Yes, I could', I lied. I've no idea if I can or can't do something till I try. 'For age 11 to 14', she went on, 'the age when they're going through it.'

I'd brought up my own six sons and two of other people's. The words 'werewolf' and 'vampire' sprang to mind, and out of my mouth. 'Brilliant', she enthused, 'and could you link them to classic books?' 'No bother', I heard myself say. 'There's *Count Dracula* and...' and I'd research werewolves, bound to be a classic there too. And that was it, a done deal. I asked my usual question when writing for schools. 'Can I write them in Scots?' The answer was no, the plays would be networked – which means broadcast throughout the UK – so English it would have to be. And that was that, apart from the writing, of course.

I spoke Scots before going to school. I'm angry that it wasn't taught at school, along with English. Instead, I had to learn about it for myself. A good teacher would have made that easier. When I began to write in Scots, I wanted to write the word 'breenge' but didn't know how. So I phoned my mother. She'd taught me to speak this language so she should know how to spell it. You don't spell it, she told me, you say it. Not much help that, when you want to write it down! Eventually I found the Scots language dictionaries. Why do Scottish people not know they have dictionaries of the words they speak? Why do we not know that we can speak and understand a language that is not English? Scots has some words which are like English words, just as Spanish has some which are like Portuguese. But they're different languages with different words, and used differently.

People read my work all over the world now, in many languages. I've written other plays for radio and for theatre. I've also written films and TV drama. But mostly it's for books, books of poetry, short stories and novels. My books of stories are *Wild Fire*, which has stories in English and in Scots, and *Not for Glory*, which is written in the Scots language spoken by the people of the village where it's set – the village I live in.

It's a wonderful gift to have two languages. In the broadcast version of *Silver Bullet*, I wrote in English but in a way that would sound Scottish. Alex says 'why are they not in their beds' instead of 'why are they not in bed.' Wattie says 'Not the now.' which nobody would ever say. A Scots speaker would say 'No the noo.' An English speaker might say 'Not right now.' I was cheating, making it look English but letting the actors know they'd have to speak it as Scottish people. I'm sure the producer noticed but she didn't object and the actors did a great job.

Panic is great oil for the imagination. I wrote *Silver Bullet* very quickly. It's about boys changing into men. I'd watched eight of them do that. From the oldest to the youngest, puberty lasted about 20 years in my house. Lovely little boys, one after another, sprouted hair, banged doors, and vanished outside as soon as it grew dark. With the younger ones, I got used to it. But with the first, I was mystified. Maybe I was like the mother in *Silver Bullet*, or the father. I hope young people will enjoy reading and performing it. I hope they'll see why parents get a bit strange when their children are at that age. I hope it helps them understand what their parents are going through. I hope parents who hear it will remember how hard it is to be that age, and how exciting it is, and be a bit less worried and a whole lot kinder to their teenagers.

Janet Paisley

About the author

JANET PAISLEY writes poems, plays, stories, films, radio and TV drama. She bides in a wee village in the hert o Scotland, keeps twa black cats, an writes fur weans, auld bodies an awbody in between.

When she was wee, she telt stories but ither fowk cried thaim lies. Noo they gie her prizes an awards fur daen it. Thae include *The Peggy Ramsay Award* fur the best new British play, a *Creative Scotland Award,* an a *BAFTA* best new screenwriter nomination fur her film, *Long Haul.*

Yince she was a teechur, but gied that up efter haen bairns. She brocht up her ain six sons an had twa ae ither fowks bidin wi her whiles they were teenagers. Wi aw their pals, the hoose was ay fu ae laddies, and sometimes lassies tae.

She's been writin as lang as she kin mind, an has written five books ae poetry, twa ae short stories, yin novella, yin novel, an a wheen o ither things. Noo her books hae been translated so fowk aw ower the world kin read her work in their ain language. She doesnae ay write in Scots. Maist o her writin is in English.

If ye want tae read ony mair, her poetry books are cried: *Pegasus in Flight, Biting through Skins, Alien Crop, Reading the Bones* an *Ye Cannae Win.*
Her fiction books are: *Wild Fire, Not for Glory, Wicked!* an *White Rose Rebel.*

NOTES

Publisher's Note: We have printed both the Scots and English versions of Janet Paisley's play, Silver Bullet so that you can compare them with each other – and see if you agree with the radio producer's decision…

SCENE ONE Living room Day

MEG sits in a chair reading a paper. ALEX enters.

ALEX: Whaur's that laddie? He kens I waant a haun sortin his bike!

MEG: Ehh?

ALEX: Oor Wattie. I'm hingin aboot oot there like a drip waitin tae faw.

MEG: How, is it rainin?

ALEX: Naw, it's no rainin! Fur ony sake, Meg, git yer nose oot that book, an pey heed.

MEG: He's in his room.

ALEX: So ye've no went deef.

MEG: I just waantit tae get tae the end. It's aboot this beast whit creeps aboot the hills at nicht, howlin at the moon an teerin folks thrapples oot.

ALEX: An nae doot, it'll meet a wheen o folk waantin thur throats ripped oot up oan the hills in the deid o nicht.

MEG: Och, I dinnae think they waant it tae happen.

ALEX: So whit wey are they no in thur beds?

MEG: That's richt, take the mick.

ALEX: Weel, horror stories! Dae ye no think we've got enough tae worry aboot wi oor ain horror story up that stair?

MEG: Wha, Wattie? He's sixteen. He's jist growin up.

ALEX: If he wis growin up, he'd be ootside helpin me sort his bike. I dinnae ken whit he's turnin intae.

A blood curdling howl from offstage.

MEG: *(A beat)* He's practisin.

ALEX: Practisin? Whit fur?

MEG: I dinnae ken.

A blood curdling howl from offstage again.

ALEX: Weel, he waants practise. Cry that music? It's got neither words nor tune. No like in oor day, eh? *(Sings)* Be bop a lula, she's ma baby. Be bop a lula, don't mean maybe. Be bop a lula, she's ma baby now, ma baby now, ma baby now. *(Stops singing)* Guid stuff, eh?

MEG: Aye, weel, it wis guid, yince.

WATTIE comes in. His voice is breaking and variable.

WATTIE: Wis that you singin, Da?

ALEX: Noo we ken hoo tae git you oot that room.

MEG: Cries it singin ony road.

ALEX: *(To Wattie)* Right you, yer bike.

WATTIE: Gies a meenut. *(Down)* Mam, kin I talk tae ye?

MEG: Course, son. Whit aboot?

WATTIE: No the noo. Efter. Aboot *(Hesitates)* stuff.

ALEX: Stuff! Ye dinnae talk tae yer mither aboot stuff. If ye waant tae talk aboot stuff, ye talk tae me.

WATTIE: You'll no like it.

ALEX: I'm no supposed tae like it. I'm yer faither. I'm supposed tae say if ye kin or if ye cannae.

MEG: Whit is it ye waant tae ken, son?

WATTIE: He'll jist say no.

ALEX: No, I'll no. I'll think aboot it furst. Then I'll say no.

He laughs uproariously at own joke.

MEG: Shut up, Alex. Whit is it, Wattie?

WATTIE: Kin I git a nose ring?

ALEX: Nae chance.

WATTIE: Ye said ye'd think aboot it.

ALEX: I think quick. Pigs huv rings in thur noses. Bulls huv rings in thur noses. Folk dinnae.

WATTIE: Weel, a stud then? That'd be cool.

ALEX: Is there somethin wrang wi yer lugs?

WATTIE: If an earring's aw richt, whey no a nose stud?

ALEX: Wi yer hearin! Somethin wrang wi yer hearin'. I said no.

WATTIE: *(Leaving)* Aw, furget it.

Door slams.

MEG: Thanks fur lettin me answer him.

ALEX: *(Calls)* Hey, whit aboot this bike?

MEG: Every time. Ye dae it every time.

ALEX: Whit dae I dae?

MEG: Git his back up.

ALEX: He never yaised tae huv a back tae git up. Yaised tae be a cheery wee boy, ay wantin his da, ay unner ma feet. Yaised tae like fitba an gaun his bike! Noo it's nose rings an a racket like he'd a fermyaird up thon stair. We never see him.

MEG: He'll stey up there aw day noo.

ALEX: Weel, you tell me, whit is he turnin intae?

Loud wolf howl from offstage.

SCENE TWO Living room Early evening

MEG sits listening to radio, cup of tea in saucer at her feet.
ALEX reads the paper.

RADIO: *(Storyteller is Alex with heavy Vincent Price horror voice)* It was the night of the full moon. Roderick stared in horror at his hands. Thick dark hair sprouted all over them. As he watched, his fingernails grew long and sharp. His body hunched over. Under his shirt, his skin prickled as the hair grew and spread.

It was happening again. Dark thoughts filled his head. Dark desires flooded his heart. He had to get out. He wanted to be where he could run free in the hills, to prowl the forests, to hunt. He wanted to throw his head back and howl with joy. He wanted the taste of blood.

ALEX: Git that rubbish aff.

He switches radio off.

MEG: Alex, I wis listenin tae that. It's aboot werewolves.

ALEX: Werewolves! Ye'd believe onythin, you. Blokes turnin intae wolves? Hing oan, I'll turn intae a wolf fur ye.

He growls, ravishing her as she squeals and giggles

MEG: *(Giggling)* Alex, gaunae stop it!

ALEX: Git awa, ye like it. I'm turnin intae a wolf. I'm a wolf!

A spine-chilling wolf howl from offstage. Cup clatters over in saucer, spilling tea.

ALEX: Whit wis that?

MEG: It wis ma tea. Ye cawed ma cup ower.

ALEX: No yer tea. Thon noise. Did ye no hear it?

MEG: Whit a mess. Skailed everywhaur. Ma guid carpet.

ALEX: Wid ye stoap faffing aboot the carpet. Whit was that howlin?

MEG: It's jist Wattie.

ALEX: It wis a wolf howl.

MEG: Ye're imaginin things. He's been daen that fur weeks.

ALEX: Howlin like thon?

MEG: Ye've heard him afore.

ALEX: I didnae realise it wis a wolf howl afore. *(Opens door, calls)* Wattie! Git yersell doon here. Right noo!

MEG: Kin ye no leave him be. Whit are ye gaunae say, stoap howlin like a wolf?

ALEX: Dinnae be daft.

WATTIE batters into the room.

WATTIE: Did ye shout me, Da? Whit is it?

ALEX: Stoap that wolf howlin, you.

MEG: So I'm daft, um I?

WATTIE: Whit're you guys oan aboot?

ALEX: You, thon racket. I waant it stoapt. An hae a shave.

WATTIE: I shaved last week.

ALEX: Weel, shave again. Men shave every day.

MEG: It widnae make ony difference tae him.

WATTIE: I'm no a man onyroad.

ALEX: An stoap daen that wi yer vyce. Up, doon, up doon.

WATTIE: Weel, I wid if I could but I cannae! Och, I'm gaun oot.

He exits.

ALEX: *(Calls after him)* Here you, if ye're no a man, whit are ye, eh? Eh? *(To Meg)* See, nae answer.

MEG: Dae ye wonder?

ALEX: Aye, I wonder. I wonder whey he's tryin tae fricht us wi aw this werewolf nonsense.

He exits upstage and opens the curtains

MEG: He never said owt aboot werewolves. Whit are ye openin the curtains fur?

ALEX: I waant tae see whaur he goes. He never gangs oot in the daylicht. Only if it's pitch daurk. Pit that licht oot, will ye?

MEG: This is stupit. *(Switches off light)* There, ae ye happy noo?

ALEX: Naw, I'm no.

MEG: Alex, whit's wrang? Whit's he daen? Kin ye see?

ALEX: Naw, I cannae see him. He must've run.

MEG: Whit rubbish ye talk. He cannae be ootae sicht awready. Whit's he goat, fower legs?

ALEX: Meg. Meg. Wid ye luik at that!

MEG: Whit?

ALEX: The moon. Thon muckle bricht full moon up thonder.

From far in the distance a wolf howl.

SCENE THREE Wattie's bedroom Early evening

WATTIE lies in bed. He is in shadow and we cannot see him clearly. He grunts as though struggling with something. There is a knocking on the door.

MEG: *(Voice off)* Wattie, open this door.

WATTIE: *(Alarmed)* Mam!

MEG: *(Voice off)* I jist waant a word wi ye, son.

WATTIE: *(Struggling with something)* Haud oan a meenut. *(Down, to himself)* Och, come oan! *(Up, to Meg)* Hing oan.

He slaps and lumps up a pillow.

WATTIE: *(Down, to himself)* Richt. *(Up, to Meg)* Jist comin.

> *He opens the door.*

MEG: Son, ae you aw richt?

WATTIE: Aye. How?

MEG: Jist, ye've been actin awfy funny.

WATTIE: Weel, I've been feelin a bit funny.

MEG: Like how?

WATTIE: Ma vyce brekin an that.

MEG: Aye, so it is. Must feel awfy peculiar.

WATTIE: Dinnae suppose it ever happened tae you.

MEG: No so's I noticed. Whaur'd ye go last night, when ye went oot?

WATTIE: Naewhaur. Hingin aboot, that's aw.

MEG: Meet onybody, did ye?

WATTIE: *(Nervous laugh)* No so's I noticed. Mam, kin I ask ye somethin?

MEG: Onythin, son. Onythin at aw.

WATTIE: Hoo d'ye git rid o hair?

MEG: *(Horrified)* Hair? *(Recovers)* Aw, ye mean like shavin.

WATTIE: No ma face.

MEG: Whit then? No yer heid!

WATTIE: Naw. I mean, weel, like, dae you shave yer legs?

MEG: Naw. I'd cut masell. I yaise special cream, jist in the summer, mind. Fur the holidays. It's in the bathroom.

WATTIE: Aw, right. An kin ye yaise it fur ither bits, like hauns an airms an chists?

MEG: I dinnae huv hair oan ma chist! Wattie, whit is this aw aboot?

WATTIE: I jist waantit tae ken.

MEG: Dae ye think I'm stupit? Somethin's gaun oan. Somethin's no richt. Whit is it?

WATTIE: I cannae tell ye, Mam. Ye'd jist worry. An ma da'd go ballistic.

MEG: Yer da's gaun ballistic awready. Wattie, ye cannae keep secrets.

WATTIE: I'm no tellin ye!

SCENE FOUR Living room Early evening

ALEX sits listening to the radio.

RADIO: *(The speaker is MEG but as a learned professor, perhaps with Germanic or Swiss accent)* Lycanthropy is a rare disease where the patient thinks they are becoming a wolf. They avoid daylight, preferring the wolf-time of darkness. They crouch and run on all fours. The only food they will accept is raw meat. There is a liking for the taste of blood. Sufferers of the condition grunt and growl. Howling is common. The notion of being a wolf is, however, all in the person's imagination. Werewolves, on the other hand...

ALEX turns off the radio as MEG enters.

MEG: Whit's that ye were listenin tae?

ALEX: A programme.

MEG: Must've been guid. Ye switched it aff.

ALEX: They'll repeat it. Whit did he say?

MEG: He waants tae git rid o hair. Fae aw ower his body. Legs, airms, chist. His hauns even!

ALEX: I kent it! He's turnin intae a werewolf, richt enough.

MEG: He's oor laddie, Alex.

ALEX: No ony mair. Luik at whit he does, howlin.

MEG: Practisin, he says.

ALEX: Practisin whit, howlin?

MEG: I didnae ask whit.

ALEX: He's ay growlin. Ay squeakin. Hides awa in his room aw the time 'less there's a full moon, then he's aff oot. Says he's no a man. An noo the hair. Weel, that's it.

MEG: Alex, whaur ae ye gaun?

ALEX: I'm gaunae tell him. There'll be nae turnin intae a werewolf in ma hoose.

MEG: Ye cannae tell him that.

ALEX: Try an stoap me.

MEG: Ye're ower late!

ALEX: Hoo d'ye mean, ower late?

MEG: Luik at thur!

ALEX: A pair ae tights?

MEG: They're aw ripped. Luik at thum!

ALEX: So ye tore yer tights.

MEG: They were in oor Wattie's room, shoved unner his pilla.

ALEX: He tore yer tights?

MEG: They're no ma tights. I dinnae weer that kind. Or that colour.

ALEX: Ye mean they're somebody else's tights? But wha?

MEG: He widnae say. Jist pit a face oan like he didnae ken.

ALEX: Richt, that's it! That is definitely it!

MEG: Whaur ae ye gaun noo?

ALEX: I'm gaunae git him telt. There will be nae ripping up tights in ma hoose!

MEG: Alex, it's no the tights!

ALEX: Then whit is it?

MEG: It's wha wis weerin thum. Whaur is she?

ALEX: Aw, naw.

MEG: See? She micht be lyin up oan thae hills wi...*(Stops)*

ALEX: *(Finishes for her)*...wi her thrapple torn oot.

MEG: Whit are we gaunae dae?

From offstage a wolf howl.

SCENE FIVE Living room Next evening

MEG is standing by the window. ALEX enters.

MEG: Whaur've ye been? I've been worrit seik.

ALEX: Gettin the necessaries.

MEG: Yer programme's oan. Thon repeat.

ALEX: Programme! We're livin it. Is he still in?

MEG: Kin ye no tell?

From offstage a wolf howl.

MEG: He's been gettin mair an mair worked up. Pacin aboot.
Clatterin an bangin. He's gettin ready tae gang oot,
I'm shair. I didnae ken if I could stoap him.

ALEX: Aw, we'll stoap him, aw richt. Here we are. *(Pulls a gun from his pocket)* Yin gun.

MEG: A gun!

ALEX: A pistol.

MEG: Still a gun.

ALEX: It's a tattie gun.

MEG: Whey wid onybody shoot tatties?

ALEX: Naebody shoots tatties. You poke the barrel intae a tattie an it loads a wee plug.

MEG: Ye're gaunae stoap a werewolf wi a wee daud ae tattie!

ALEX: I'm no gaunae stoap him. You are.

MEG: Me?

ALEX: You're his mither. You hud him. You kin sort him oot.

MEG: I'm no shootin oor Wattie. No even wi a daud ae tattie.

ALEX: It's no Wattie. No noo. It's a werewolf. An it's no a daud ae tattie.

He fires it into the chair.

MEG: That went richt through ma cushion!

ALEX: Aye.

MEG: Ma guid cushion cover!

ALEX: It's a special bullet. I made it.

MEG: Bullet!

ALEX: A silver bullet. That's hoo ye stoap a werewolf. Wi a silver bullet.

MEG: Weel, it's somewhaur inside ma cushion noo.

ALEX: I've got anither yin. Will ye stoap faffing aboot ower yer cushion? Here, take the gun.

He hands her the gun.

MEG: Jings, it's heavy, in't it?

ALEX: Aye. An here's the ither bullet.

MEG: It's tottie.

ALEX: Weel, excuse me but the local silver mine wis shut!

MEG: Take the mick, whey din't ye? Time like this. That's jist typical ae you.

ALEX: It doesnae huv tae be a big bullet. It jist needs tae be silver an inside him!

MEG: I could've hid it in his mince. Then it wid've been inside him.

ALEX: Ye hae tae shoot him wi it. Ae ye daft?

MEG: He widnae've seen it in the mince. He'll see the gun.

ALEX: Aye, an then ye'll shoot him.

MEG: You shair this is legal?

ALEX: Of coorse it's legal. Ye dinnae think I'd let ye shoot oor laddie wi an illegal gun, dae ye? I bocht it fae the post office.

MEG: I mean shootin him.

ALEX: Is it legal tae turn intae a werewolf, ask yersell that!

MEG: Aw richt, aw richt.

ALEX: Weel, oan ye go then.

Door creaks open.

MEG: Eh, whit aboot you?

ALEX: I'm yer back-up.

MEG: Back-up?

ALEX: If ye miss, I'll gang an git the polis.

MEG: Whit'll Wattie dae if I miss?

As they exit.

ALEX: He'll… mibbe he'll… or he micht… Look, dinnae miss.

RADIO: *(The professor continues)* Werewolves, on the other hand, come from other people's imaginations. In early times, villagers often ate bread made from mouldy flour. The mould made people see things that weren't there. If one man saw another begin to turn into a wolflike creature and told the others then, like hypnosis, they'd begin to see what he'd suggested. Someone else might see the creature grab a child. The others would see it too. If someone shouted 'now he's eating her', they'd all see that happen. After the effects of the mould had worn off, the werewolf man, or woman, would be burnt to death. But he would have done nothing. It was all in the villagers' imaginations.

SCENE SIX Wattie's bedroom Evening

It is dark apart from the moonlight coming in through a window. We can see the outline of WATTIE in the shadows, There is a wolf howl reminiscent of 'Blue Moon'.

Sound of door clattering open. MEG enters with ALEX behind her.

WATTIE: Is that you, mam? Mam!

MEG: Wattie?

WATTIE: I didnae waant ye seein me lookin like this.

MEG: It's daurk, son. Lookin like whit?

WATTIE walks into the light. He is wearing a dress.

MEG: Whey are ye weerin a frock?

WATTIE: Whey are you pintin a gun at me?

MEG: Ye've got tights oan. An make-up.

WATTIE: I kin explain.

ALEX: It's a disguise. He doesnae waant us tae ken.

WATTIE: That's no a real gun, is it?

ALEX: Real enough. Ye're ower late, we ken awready!

WATTIE: Da, please.

ALEX: Dae it noo, Meg!

MEG: I cannae. He looks funny.

ALEX: He'll look mair funny in a meenut when the hair sprouts! Shoot him!

WATTIE: Dinnae, Mam. I huv tae go oot.

MEG: I cannae let ye, Wattie.

ALEX: Afore he gits awa! Shoot!

WATTIE: Dinnae, mam. Dinnae shoot me, please.

MEG: It's fur yer ain guid.

ALEX: Shoot!

The pistol fires with a crack.

WATTIE: *(Yells)* Ahhh!

ALEX: Ye goat him!

WATTIE: *(Yells)* Owww!

ALEX: He's howlin. Shoot him again.

MEG: Ye only gied me wan bullet!

WATTIE: *(Yells)* Ma-amm

MEG drops the gun.

MEG: Aw, Wattie! Ae ye aw richt?

WATTIE: *(Yells)* Owww! I've been shot!

MEG: I'm sorry. Wattie, speak tae me.

WATTIE: Ahhh! I wid've telt ye aboot the dressin up. Owww! It's fur the schule play. But I kent ye'd be mad.

ALEX: Howlin like a wolf fur the schule play?

WATTIE: I wis tryin tae keep ma vyce high. It kept oan brekin.

MEG: Whit aboot the hair ye waantit rid o, fae yer legs, yer airms, yer hauns?

WATTIE: I'm supposed tae be a lassie. They dinnae hae aw that. No like I huv.

ALEX: Ye were playin a lassie!

WATTIE: I didnae think ye'd be mad enough tae shoot me. Owww! That hit the side ae ma nose. Ye could've blinded me, mam!

MEG: I ken. I'm really sorry.

WATTIE: I've goat a lump. There's a wee lump stuck oan ma nose.

MEG: That's the silver plug. It's sparklin.

WATTIE: Silver? Sparklin. Gie me that mirror ower. Let me see.

MEG: *(Down, to ALEX)* The schule play!

ALEX: *(Down, to MEG)* Easy mistake tae make. *(Up)* Faffing aboot. There's no even yin drop ae blood.

WATTIE: Hey, look at ma nose. Is that the business! A nose stud! Is that cool or whit? A nose-piercin gun. I wish ye'd telt me. Near frichted me tae daith there.

MEG: Weel, I didnae, kinna, think.

WATTIE: Ta, Mam. Ye're a real pal.

ALEX: Eh, it wis aw ma idea.

WATTIE: Then ye dinnae mind aboot the play, me haen tae dress like a lassie?

ALEX: Naw. Naw. Could be *(Beat)* worse.

MEG: *(To Alex)* Your idea?

ALEX: The gun. The silver…

MEG: Bullet!

WATTIE: Hey, I've goat tae go. We're oan stage in hauf an hoor. See tights, Mam? I dinnae ken hoo ye git thae things oan. I kept tearin thum. There's tickets by ma bed if yeese waant tae come. Wait tae the guys see this. Nose stud, eh? Eat yer hert oot, Becks. Hoo cool am I?

He exits howling with wolf-like delight.

MEG: Werewolf, is it?

ALEX: You started it.

MEG growls.

ALEX: *(Backing away from her)* Noo, Meg...

MEG growls.

ALEX: Stey back. Git awa fae ma throat. Meg!

As the lights go down to blackout we can hear their growls and squeals.

SCENE SEVEN Living room Evening

A spotlight comes up on the radio.

RADIO: *(The voice is Wattie, as the programme presenter)* Of, course, Professor, nothing has yet been been proved. But with so many werewolf stories throughout history, and today, some may well be true.

Prolonged, euphoric Wolf Howl. Lights dim to blackout.

END OF PLAY

SCENE ONE Living room Day

MEG sits reading. ALEX enters.

ALEX: Have you seen that boy? He was supposed to give me a hand fixing his bike!

MEG: Mmm?

ALEX: Our Wattie. I'm hanging about out there like a drip waiting to fall.

MEG: Why, is it raining?

ALEX: No, it isn't raining. For goodness sake, Meg, get your nose out of that book and pay attention.

MEG: He's in his room.

ALEX: So you did hear me.

MEG: I just wanted to get to the end. It's about this beast that wanders the hills at night, howling at the moon and tearing people's throats out.

ALEX: And I suppose this beast meets a lot of people wanting their throats ripped out up on the hills in the dead of night?

MEG: Oh, I don't think they want it to happen.

ALEX: Then why aren't they all in bed?

MEG: That's right, take the mick.

ALEX: Well, horror stories! Don't you think we've got enough to worry about with our own horror story upstairs.

MEG: Who, Wattie? He's sixteen. He's just growing up.

ALEX: If he was growing up, he'd be outside helping me fix his bike. I don't know what he's turning into.

A blood curdling howl from offstage.

MEG: *(A beat)* He's practising.

ALEX: Practising? For what?

MEG: I don't know.

A blood curdling howl from offstage again.

ALEX: He needs practice. Music these days. It's got neither words nor tune. Not like in our day, eh? *(Sings)* Be bop a lula, she's ma baby. Be bop a lula, don't mean maybe. Be bop a lula, she's ma baby now, ma baby now, ma baby now. *(Stops singing)* Good stuff, eh?

MEG: Yeh, well it was good.

WATTIE comes in. His voice is breaking and variable.

WATTIE: Was that you singing, Dad?

ALEX: Now we know how to get you out of that room.

MEG: Calls it singing anyway.

ALEX: *(To Wattie)* Right you, your bike.

WATTIE: In a minute. *(Down)* Mum, can I talk to you?

MEG: Course, son. What about?

WATTIE: Not just now. After. About *(Hesitates)* stuff.

ALEX: Stuff! You don't talk to your mother about stuff. If you want to talk about stuff, it's me you talk to.

WATTIE: You won't like it.

ALEX: I'm not supposed to like it. I'm your dad. I'm supposed to tell you if you can or can't.

MEG: What is it you want to ask me, son?

WATTIE: He'll just say no.

ALEX: No, I won't. I'll think about it first. Then I'll say no.

He laughs uproariously at own joke.

MEG: Shut up, Alex. What is it, Wattie?

WATTIE: Can I get a nose ring?

ALEX: No chance.

WATTIE: You said you'd think about it.

ALEX: I think quick. Pigs have rings in their noses. Bulls have rings in their noses. People don't.

WATTIE: Well, a stud then? That would be cool.

ALEX: Is there something wrong with your ears?

WATTIE: If an earring's all right, why not a nose stud?

ALEX: With your hearing! Something wrong with your hearing. I said no.

WATTIE: *(Leaving)* Oh, forget it.

> *Door slams.*

MEG: Glad you let me answer him.

ALEX: *(Calls)* Hey, what about this bike?

MEG: Every time. You do it every time.

ALEX: What did I do?

MEG: Get his back up.

ALEX: He never used to have a back to get up. Used to be a happy little boy, always wanting his dad, always under my feet. Used to be interested in playing football and riding his bike! Now it's nose rings and a racket like he'd a jungle upstairs. We never see him.

MEG: He'll stay up in his room all day now.

ALEX: Well, you tell me, what is he turning into?

> *Loud wolf howl from upstairs.*

SCENE TWO Living room Early evening

MEG sits listening to radio, cup of tea in saucer at her feet.
ALEX reads the paper.

RADIO: *(Storyteller is ALEX with heavy Vincent Price horror voice)*
It was the night of the full moon. Roderick stared in
horror at his hands. Thick dark hair sprouted all over
them. As he watched, his fingernails grew long and sharp.
His body hunched over. Under his shirt, his skin prickled
as the hair grew and spread.

It was happening again. Dark thoughts filled his head.
Dark desires flooded his heart. He had to get out. He
wanted to be where he could run free in the hills, to prowl
the forests, to hunt. He wanted to throw his head back
and howl with joy. He wanted the taste of blood.

ALEX: Get that rubbish off.

He switches radio off.

MEG: Alex, I was listening to that. It's about werewolves.

ALEX: Werewolves! You'd believe anything, you. Men turning
into wolves. Here, I'll turn into a wolf for you.

He growls, ravishing her as she squeals and giggles.

MEG: *(Giggling)* Alex, stop it!

ALEX: Get away, you like it. I'm turning into a wolf. I'm a wolf!

A spine-chilling wolf howl from offstage. Cup clatters over in
saucer, spilling tea.

ALEX: What was that?

MEG: It was my tea. You've knocked it over.

ALEX: Not your tea. That noise. Did you hear it?

MEG: Look at the mess. My good carpet.

ALEX: Will you stop fussing about the carpet. What was that
howling?

MEG: It's only Wattie.

ALEX: It was only a wolf howl.

MEG: You're imagining things. He's been doing that for weeks.

ALEX: Howling like that?

MEG: You've heard him before.

ALEX: I never noticed it was a wolf howl before.

He opens door.

ALEX: *(Calls)* Wattie! Get down here. This minute!

MEG: Can't you leave him be. What are you going to say to him this time? Stop howling like a wolf?

ALEX: Don't be stupid.

WATTIE batters into the room.

WATTIE: Did you shout for me, Dad? What is it?

ALEX: Stop that wolf howling, you.

MEG: So I'm stupid, am I?

WATTIE: What're you guys on about?

ALEX: You, that racket. I want it stopped. And take a shave.

WATTIE: I shaved last week.

ALEX: Well, shave again. Men shave every day.

MEG: It wouldn't make any difference to him.

WATTIE: I'm not a man anyway.

ALEX: And stop doing that with your voice. Up, down, up, down.

WATTIE: Well, I would if I could but I can't! Oh, I'm going out.

He exits.

ALEX: *(Calls after him)* And if you're not a man, what are you, eh? Eh? *(To MEG)* See, no answer.

MEG: Are you surprised?

ALEX: That my son's trying to spook us with this werewolf nonsense?

He exits Upstage and opens the curtains

MEG: He never mentioned werewolves. Why are you opening the curtains?

ALEX: I want to see where he went. He never goes out in the daylight. Just when it's pitch dark. Put that light out, will you?

MEG: This is ridiculous. *(Switches off light)* There, are you happy now?

ALEX: No.

MEG: Alex, what's wrong? What is he doing? Can you see?

ALEX: No, I can't see him. He must've run.

MEG: The rubbish you talk. He can't be out of sight already. What's he got, four legs?

ALEX: Meg. Meg. Would you look at that!

MEG: What?

ALEX: That moon. That big white full moon up there.

From far in the distance a wolf howl.

SCENE THREE Wattie's bedroom
Early evening

WATTIE lies in bed. He is in shadow and we cannot see him clearly. He grunts as though struggling with something. There is a knocking on the door.

MEG: *(Voice off)* Wattie, open the door.

WATTIE: *(Alarmed)* Mum!

MEG: *(Voice off)* I just want to talk to you, son.

WATTIE: *(Struggling with something)* Wait a minute. *(Down, to himself)*: Oh, come on! *(Up, to Meg)* Just a minute.

He slaps and lumps up a pillow.

WATTIE: *(Down, to himself)* Right. *(Up, to Meg)* Just coming.

He opens the door.

MEG: Son, are you all right?

WATTIE: I'm fine.

MEG: Just, you've been acting a bit strange recently.

WATTIE: Well, I've been feeling a bit strange.

MEG: In what way?

WATTIE: My voice breaking and stuff.

MEG: Yeh, I've noticed that. Must make you feel peculiar.

WATTIE: Don't suppose it ever happened to you.

MEG: Not that I noticed. Where did you go last night, when you went out?

WATTIE: Nowhere special. Just hanging out, you know.

MEG: Meet anybody, did you?

WATTIE: *(Nervous laugh)* Not that I noticed. Mum, can I ask you something?

MEG: Anything, son. Anything at all.

WATTIE: How d'you get rid of hair?

MEG: *(Horrified)* Hair? *(Recovers)* Oh, you mean like shaving.

WATTIE: Not my face.

MEG: What then? Not your head!

WATTIE: No. I mean, well like, do you shave your legs?

MEG: No. I'd cut myself. I use special cream, just in the summertime. For the holidays. It's in the bathroom.

WATTIE: Right. And is that good for other places, like hands and arms and chests.

MEG: I don't have hair on my chest! Wattie, what is all this about?

WATTIE: I only wanted to know.

MEG: Do you think I'm stupid? Something's up. Something's bothering you. What is it?

WATTIE: I can't tell you, Mum. You'd only worry. And my dad would be annoyed.

MEG: Your dad's already annoyed. Wattie, you can't keep secrets.

WATTIE: I'm not telling you!

SCENE FOUR Living room Early evening

ALEX sits listening to the radio,

RADIO: *(The speaker is MEG but as a learned professor, perhaps with Germanic or Swiss accent)* Lycanthropy is a rare disease where the patient thinks they are becoming a wolf. They avoid daylight, preferring the wolf-time of darkness. They crouch and run on all fours. The only food they will accept is raw meat. There is a liking for the taste of blood. Sufferers of the condition grunt and growl. Howling is common. The notion of being a wolf is, however, all in the person's imagination. Werewolves, on the other hand...

ALEX turns off the radio as MEG enters.

MEG: What was that you were listening to?

ALEX: A programme.

MEG: Must've been good. You switched it off.

ALEX: It'll be repeated. What did he say?

MEG: He wants to get rid of hair. From all over his body. Legs, arms, chest. His hands even!

ALEX: So that's it then. He's turning into a werewolf.

MEG: He's our son, Alex.

ALEX: Look at the evidence. He howls.

MEG: Practising, he said.

ALEX: Practising what? Howling?

MEG: I didn't ask what.

ALEX: He growls. He squeaks. He hides in his room all the time. Except when there's a full moon, then he's off out. He says he's not a man. And now the hair. Well, that's it.

MEG: Alex, where are you going?

ALEX: I'm going to tell him. There will be no turning into a werewolf in my house.

MEG: You can't tell him that.

ALEX: Stop me.

MEG: It's too late!

ALEX: How d'you mean, too late.

MEG: Look!

ALEX: A pair of tights?

MEG: They're ripped to shreds. Look at them!

ALEX: So you ripped your tights.

MEG: They were in Wattie's room. Hidden under his pillow.

ALEX: He ripped your tights?

MEG: They're not my tights. I don't wear that kind. Or that colour.

ALEX: They're somebody else's tights! Whose?

MEG: He wouldn't say. Just shrugged and looked puzzled.

ALEX: Right, that's it! That is definitely it!

MEG: Where're you going now!

ALEX: I'm going to tell him. There'll be no ripping up tights in my house!

MEG: Alex, it's not the tights!

ALEX: Then what is it?

MEG: It's who was wearing them. Where is she?

ALEX: Oh, my goodness.

MEG: See? She could be lying up on the hills with...*(Stops)*

ALEX: *(Finishes for her)* ...with her throat ripped out.

MEG: What are we going to do?

From offstage a wolf howl.

SCENE FIVE Living room Next evening

MEG is standing by the window. ALEX enters.

MEG: Where've you been? I've been worried sick.

ALEX: Getting the necessaries.

MEG: Your programme's on. The repeat.

ALEX: Programme! We're living it. Is he still in?

MEG: Can't you tell?

From offstage a wolf howl.

MEG: He's been getting more and more excited. Pacing about. Rattling and banging. He's getting ready to go out. I'm sure of it. I didn't know if I could stop him.

ALEX: Oh, we'll stop him, all right. Here it is. *(Pulls gun from his pocket)* One gun.

MEG: A gun!

ALEX: A pistol.

MEG: Still a gun.

ALEX: It's a potato gun.

MEG: Why would anybody shoot potatoes?

ALEX: Nobody shoots potatoes. You push the barrel into a potato and it loads a little plug.

MEG: You're going to stop a werewolf with a little plug of potato!

ALEX: I'm not going to stop him. You are.

MEG: Me?

ALEX: You're his mother. You had him. You can sort him out.

MEG: I'm not shooting our Wattie. Not even with a piece of potato.

ALEX: It's not Wattie. Not any more. It's a werewolf. And it's not a piece of potato.

ALEX fires into the chair.

MEG: That went right through the cushion!

ALEX: Yip.

MEG: My good cushion cover!

ALEX: It's a special bullet! I made it.

MEG: Bullet!

ALEX: A silver bullet. That's how you stop a werewolf. With a silver bullet.

MEG: Well, it's somewhere inside the cushion now.

ALEX: I've got another one. Will you stop fussing about over that cushion? Here, take the gun.

He hands her the gun.

MEG: Oh, it's heavy, isn't it?

ALEX: Yip. And here's the other bullet.

MEG: It's tiny.

ALEX: Well, excuse me but the local silver mine was closed!

MEG: Take the mick, why don't you?. Time like this. That's just typical of you.

ALEX: It doesn't have to be a big bullet. It just has to be silver and inside him!

MEG: I could've hidden it in his mince. Then it would've been inside him.

ALEX: You have to shoot him with it. Are you stupid?

MEG: He wouldn't have seen it in the mince. He'll notice the gun.

ALEX: Yeh, and then you'll shoot him.

MEG: Is this legal?

ALEX: Of course it's legal. You don't think I'd let you shoot our son with an illegal gun, do you? I bought it in the post office.

MEG: I meant shooting him.

ALEX: Is it legal to turn into a werewolf, ask yourself that!

MEG: All right, all right.

ALEX: Well, on you go then.

Door creaks open.

MEG: Eh, what about you?

ALEX: I'm your back-up.

MEG: Back-up?

ALEX: If you miss, I'll go and get the police.

MEG: What'll Wattie do if I miss?

As they exit.

ALEX: He'll... maybe he'll... or he could... Look, don't miss.

RADIO: *(The professor continues)* Werewolves, on the other hand, come from other people's imaginations. In early times, villagers often ate bread made from mouldy flour. The mould made people see things that weren't there. If one man saw another begin to turn into a wolflike creature and told the others then, like hypnosis, they'd begin to see what he'd suggested. Someone else might see the creature grab a child. The others would see it too. If someone shouted 'now he's eating her', they'd all see that happen. After the effects of the mould had worn off, the werewolf man, or woman, would be burnt to death. But he would have done nothing. It was all in the villagers' imaginations.

SCENE SIX Wattie's bedroom Evening

It is dark apart from the moonlight coming in through a window. We can see the outline of WATTIE in the shadows. There is a wolf howl reminiscent of 'Blue Moon'.

Door clatters open. MEG enters with ALEX behind her.

WATTIE: Mum!

MEG: Wattie?

WATTIE: I didn't want you to see me looking like this.

MEG: You look, you look...

WATTIE walks into the light. He is wearing a dress.

MEG: Why are you wearing a dress?

WATTIE: Why are you pointing a gun at me?

MEG: You've got tights on. And make-up.

WATTIE: I can explain.

ALEX: It's a disguise. He doesn't want us to guess.

WATTIE: That isn't a real gun, is it?

ALEX: Real enough. You're too late, we guessed!

WATTIE: Dad, please.

ALEX: Do it now, Meg!

MEG: I can't. He looks funny.

ALEX: He'll look even funnier in a minute when the hair sprouts! Shoot him!

WATTIE: Don't, Mum. I have to go out.

MEG: I can't let you, Wattie.

ALEX: Before he gets away! Shoot!

WATTIE: Don't, mum. Don't shoot me, please.

MEG: It's for your own good.

ALEX: Shoot!

>   *The pistol fires with a crack.*

WATTIE: *(Yells)* Ahhh!

ALEX: You got him!

WATTIE: *(Yells)* Owww!

ALEX: He's howling. Shoot him again.

MEG: You only gave me one bullet!

WATTIE: *(Yells)* Mu-umm

>   *MEG drops the gun.*

MEG: Oh, Wattie! Are you all right?

WATTIE: *(Yells)* Owww! I've been shot!

MEG: I'm sorry. Wattie, speak to me.

WATTIE: Ahhh! I would've told you about the dressing up. Owww! It's for the school play. But I knew you'd be mad.

ALEX: Howling like a wolf for the school play?

WATTIE: I was trying to keep my voice high. It kept breaking.

MEG: What about the hair you wanted rid of, from your legs, your arms, your hands?

WATTIE: I'm supposed to play a girl. They don't have all that. Not like I have.

ALEX: You were playing a girl!

WATTIE: I didn't think you'd be mad enough to shoot me. Owww! It hit the side of my nose. You could've blinded me, mum!

MEG: I know. I'm really sorry.

WATTIE: I've got a lump. There's a wee lump stuck on my nose.

MEG: That's the silver plug. It's sparkling.

WATTIE: Silver? Sparkling. Give me that mirror over. Let me see.

MEG: *(Down, to ALEX)* The school play!

ALEX: *(Down, to MEG)* Easy mistake to make. *(Up)* Fuss about nothing. There's not even a drop of blood.

WATTIE: Hey, look at my nose. Is that the business! A nose stud! Is that cool or what? A nose-piercing gun. I wish you'd told me. Nearly frightened me to death there.

MEG: Well, I didn't, sort of, think.

WATTIE: Thanks, Mum. You're a real pal.

ALEX: Eh, it was my idea.

WATTIE: Then you don't mind about the play, me having to dress like a girl?

ALEX: No. No. Could be *(Beat)* worse.

MEG: *(To ALEX)* Your idea?

ALEX: The gun. The silver...

MEG: Bullet!

WATTIE: Hey, I've got to go. We're on stage in half an hour. See tights, Mum? I don't know how you get them on. I kept tearing them. There's tickets beside my bed if you want to come. Wait till the guys see this. Nose stud, eh? Eat your heart out, Becks. How cool am I?

He exits howling with wolf-like delight.

MEG: Werewolf, is it?

ALEX: You started it.

MEG growls.

ALEX: Now, Meg.

MEG growls.

ALEX: Stay back. Get away from my throat. Meg!

As the lights go down to blackout we can hear their growls and squeals.

SCENE SEVEN Living room Evening

A spotlight comes up on the radio.

RADIO: *(The voice is WATTIE as the programme presenter)* Of, course, Professor, nothing has yet been been proved. But with so many werewolf stories throughout history, and today, some may well be true.

Prolonged, euphoric wolf howl. Lights dim to blackout.

END OF PLAY

ACTIVITIES

Close reading

Understanding

1 List, in chronological order, the main events and incidents of the play. Highlight the most important. Summarise the plot in no more than five sentences.

2 Reread scenes 4 and 5 in either version of *Silver Bullet*. Give the following information:

- the definition of lycanthropy

- an 'explanation' for the condition.

Analysis

Describe the relationship between Meg and Alex. Justify your answer with close reference to the text.

Evaluation

Evaluate how well the extracts from the radio programme add to:

- your understanding of the story

- the humorous tone.

Flash fiction

Write down your five favourite Scots words on a separate sheet of paper.

Then fold them up and put them into a container along with the words of everyone else in the class.

Pull five words out of the container.

Write a 500 word short story or drama script in which you use each of the words you chose at least once.

The rules

One of the words must be used in the title.

One of the words must be used in the opening sentence.

One of the words must be used in the last sentence.

Letter

I asked my usual question when writing for schools. Can I write them in Scots? The answer was no, the plays would be networked – which means broadcast throughout the UK – so English it would have to be.

With two or three others, list all television and radio characters and personalities who use a language other than English or a dialect. Highlight those that use a Scottish language or dialect.

Then still in your group, study TV and radio listings and list all programmes that are broadcast in a language other than English or a dialect. You should look at both terrestrial and satellite channels.

Use a different colour or symbol to highlight each of the following features:

- subtitles
- networked
- uses a range of dialects or languages
- uses a Scottish language or dialect.

Draw some conclusions about what you have found out.

Then on your own, write a letter to the BBC headquarters in London in which you make a case for or against the networking of programmes in a Scottish/other language or dialect.

Between the Lines

by
Alison Clark

CHARACTERS

KATHY McLEOD

ALLY McLEOD, *her husband*

IAN McLEOD, *their elder son, (17)*
a Private in the Army training as a mechanic

JANIS McLEOD, *their daughter (15)*

THOMAS McLEOD, *their younger son (11)*

SHARON, IAN'S *girlfriend (16)*

Alison Clark

I raided my own work for material for *Between the Lines* – authors have been recycling since writing was invented!

I've been working for about eight years on a novel which is set both in 1945 and 1990. The modern sections feature a Scottish family in which the son is about to go off to the army. I think in dialogue – and frequently talk to myself – so even in my prose writing, the characters talk a lot. This made it relatively easy to develop some of these family scenarios into an actual drama.

In *Between the Lines*, Ian has already embarked on his career in the army and the play opens as he's about to arrive home on his first leave. I changed the date to the year 2000 so that the action could be set between the two Gulf wars. I chose this because in spite of Ian's optimistic point of view that there's no immediate crisis in the world, the situation is unstable enough to worry his family and his new girlfriend. The audience, of course, knows what the characters can't yet know – that the war in Iraq will begin in 2003.

But the play is as much about how family members get on with each other – and sometimes don't. As is often the case in Scotland, affection is expressed indirectly through jokes and banter. I try to capture the way love and concern shines through even when the characters are worried or annoyed.

I am grateful to the young men of class 3BM at Dunoon Grammar School who without any preparation successfully gave the play an unrehearsed reading.

I hope you enjoy reading and performing it.

Alison Clark

About the author
Alison Clark has taught English in all sectors of the Scottish secondary education system. She has run, directed and written for school and former pupil drama groups.

Writing as Alison Watson she was commissioned by the Traverse Theatre to write **Moving In**, a play with music which ran successfully in the 1980 main season. In 2005 she won a place on the Arvon Foundation Advanced Playwriting course and was privileged to be tutored by David Harrower and David Greig. She now lives on the island of Bute and combines writing with running a consultancy in personal and team development.

Work for schools/students:
Maria Marten or Murder in the Red Barn, a new version for Eastwood High School drama group (with Alan Steele) 1971

Gatito a documentary drama, Edinburgh Festival Fringe 1974

Aunt Kate Saves the Day – a play for Primary 5 Laurel Bank School 1994

Recent successes:
'How to Stop Flogging a Dead Horse – The Business Owner's Guide to Creating Happy Endings' **www.bookshaker.com** 2006

Leaf Books short short story competition summer 2006 Highly Commended: to appear in 2007 anthology **www.leafbooks.co.uk**

Longlisted for the Cinnamon Press Novel award (1st 10,000 words) **www.cinnamonpress.com**

The date places the action between the two Gulf wars and immediately before certain regiments of the British Army were sent out as part of the NATO peacekeeping force in the Balkans.

It is the year 2000. The action takes place in the kitchen and living room of the McLeod family. The eldest son Ian is due home on his first leave from the army.

SCENE ONE Kitchen Morning

It is breakfast time in the McLeod household. KATHY at the breakfast table, JANIS rummaging in the fridge for her packed lunch.

KATHY: Ian rang last night.

JANIS: Uh-huh.

KATHY: V'you met this Sharon?

JANIS: *(Her back still turned away)* I've met Sharon, yeah.

KATHY: Going to stay at hers then is he?

JANIS: Looks like it. *(Snaps shut lunch box and exits kitchen)* I don't blame him.

KATHY stares after her and then starts to laugh. ALLY enters.

ALLY: *(Pouring himself tea)* What's funny?

KATHY: If I didn't laugh, I'd greet.

ALLY shrugs, none the wiser. Sits at kitchen table.

KATHY: Thomas! Is he up? I didn't realise the time.

ALLY: Haven't seen him – come to think of it, I could hear his Playstation.

KATHY: What? And you did nothing about it?

ALLY: I only thought of it just now – I didn't really take notice – you know how it is.

KATHY: I know how *you* are.

ALLY: And how's that then?

KATHY: Forget it.

THOMAS appears.

KATHY: And about time…have you had that computer on? You know you're not allowed it in the morning. Eat your cereal.

THOMAS does so trying to make himself as small as possible.

KATHY: Where did you get that shirt? Down the back of your bed? I laid you out a clean one.

ALLY: Oh Kathy, leave the kid alane and gie's peace.

KATHY: Whose side are you on?

ALLY: It's no aboot sides.

KATHY: No, you're right...I'm just in a state about Ian.

THOMAS: Ian? Is he comin' hame?

ALLY: Aye, he's due on leave.

KATHY: Not 'hame', 'home'.

ALLY: You're OK pal, eat your breakfast.

JANIS having forgotten her bus timetable (or something) whirls in and out.

JANIS: Peace broken out as usual!

THOMAS sticks his tongue out and gets his head lightly cuffed by ALLY.

KATHY: You gonnae change that shirt?

THOMAS: I'll miss the bus.

He races off before she can catch him. KATHY sinks down in a chair and puts her head in her hands.

ALLY: Are you gonnae tell me whit this is a' aboot?

KATHY: Oh he's due on leave right enough. He might even spend one of his eight days with *us*! *(Pause)* He's going to be staying with his girlfriend's folks.

ALLY: Oh, right.

KATHY: What d'ya mean 'oh right'? Has everyone in this family turned monosyllabic?

ALLY: Eh?

KATHY: Janis more or less told me to mind my own business. You've got nothing to say. Am I the only one who cares that he's, that he's...

ALLY: Take it easy...I'll make you some tea...this is stewed.

KATHY: He rang last night...'I'll be in Glasgow on Monday so I'll come over see you Tuesday' 'Over from where?' I said and he says, 'Sharon's' like it's dead obvious. Apparently her folks are expectin' him.

ALLY: So whit did ye say?

KATHY: Whit could ah say? It seemed to be a' settled. I just had tae accept it...I gave him a bit of an earful, mind.

ALLY: *(Smiling)* Never.

KATHY: To be fair, he did say he shoulda let me know. The thing is, are they stayin' here on Tuesday night? Or just comin' for tea?

ALLY: Wait and see. They can have the sofa bed in the front room if they want.

KATHY: I'm no sure about that.

ALLY: How no?

KATHY: You know.

ALLY: Kathy, he's in the army. He's old enough to be married and old enough to get k...(*He stops short*)

KATHY: Don't start.

ALLY: Ah wisny. Look ah'll need tae go. Hang in doll, eh
(Hands her a mug of tea)

KATHY: Listen to you.

ALLY: We'll be OK

KATHY goes over to the telephone, picks up the receiver, and punches in a number. Slight pause.

KATHY: It's me...aye. Listen I'm up tae here wi' them a'. Gonnae meet us after ma shift?... Aye, three-ish, in the caff... No more than usual, no... Well, Ian's leave's comin' up and he's stayin' with some girl I've never met, Janis has done a complete Jekyll and Hyde, and Ally...oh look I'll see you later. I'll need to put a wash on before I go.

She hangs up. She exits.

JANIS takes a mobile from her pocket and makes a call.

JANIS: Total nightmare...like livin' in a zoo... My brother's due 'is first leave and he's staying wi' the girlfriend. Maw went ballistic... Hormones? Tell me aboot it. Your whole life's a bloody hormone trip if you ask me... Naw, I'm on work experience this week. It's OK...I thought it was gonnae be dead borin' but once I got given somethin' to do, it was no bad. Whit? When? Tuesday? Naw...that's when Ian's bringin' Sharon round...and miss the fun? Naw, make it Monday.

SCENE TWO Living room Tuesday Late afternoon

The living room is empty. IAN lets himself in with his key. He enters the living room with SHARON, who looks nervous. Movement is heard from upstairs.

IAN: Mum? Hullo?...

He looks at SHARON and shrugs. After a pause KATHY appears straightening a jersey she has just pulled on.

KATHY: I was just gettin' changed...didn't expect you till later.

IAN: Sorry.

KATHY: No, no...you're fine. I was in the loft and forgot the time.

IAN: This is Sharon.

KATHY: Hullo, Sharon, come on in.

KATHY and SHARON: *(Together)* How d'you do, Mrs McLeod.

They laugh nervously and everyone goes into the kitchen.

SHARON: I'm sorry...I said to Ian we should have rung.

KATHY: No need, no need...you sit down and I'll put the kettle on. Coffee? Or there's some cans of ginger if you'd rather?

SHARON: Coffee would be lovely.

IAN fetches himself a can of coke from the fridge. KATHY makes coffee.

IAN: Am I getting' a hug or what?

KATHY: Sure. *(He envelops her)* There seems to be more of you.

IAN: Pure muscle that's what it is.

SHARON: Idiot.

IAN: What were you in the loft fur?

KATHY: I was looking at old photographs.

IAN groans.

KATHY: I'm not gonnae embarrass you. Your Gran wanted one of that last holiday we all went.

Hands SHARON a mug of coffee.

SHARON: Thanks Mrs McLeod.

KATHY: Call me Kathy.

SHARON: Right.

Nobody speaks.

KATHY: So where did you two meet?

IAN: At Robbie's twenty first. Shaz was the DJ...remember he had a party at Fozzie's last year?

KATHY: Oh yeah, before you signed up?

IAN: Aye. We'd only just started goin' out.

KATHY: And you kept in touch?

IAN: Texting an that.

SHARON: Just as well there's mobiles...don't see him as a letter writer.

IAN: Compliment me why don't you?

They laugh together, comfortable.

KATHY: I need to do something about the tea. Are you happy to sit here and give us your chat while I get on?

SHARON: If we're not in your way.

KATHY: No, no. It's just I should have started before this but I didn't realise how long I'd been up there. You know what it's like when you start finding things.

SHARON: Yeah, we flitted last year and you wouldn't believe the stuff that turned up.

KATHY: You live with your folks Sharon?

SHARON: Yeah, me and my sister. My big brother works in Newcastle.

KATHY sets about preparing the meal.

SHARON: Can I help with anything?

KATHY: You could slice some tomatoes?

SHARON: Sure.

IAN: I'll set the table.

KATHY: Well, well! They've replaced him with a new model!

Lights dim to blackout.

SCENE THREE Living room Later

Lights come up on laughter and conversation. Everyone sitting at dinner table.

IAN: So I said –

JANIS: Oh yes, big man.

IAN: I did! I says to 'im, who are you calling a teuchter bastard, sorry Ma, a teuchter so and so.

KATHY: Thank you.

IAN: He lunges at me. I do a quick sidestep and he falls face first in the trifle!

SHARON, IAN and JANIS are hooting with laughter. THOMAS is gazing in wonder. KATHY and ALLY smiling.

KATHY: So how is it really Ian? You look okay.

IAN: I *am* okay, Mum, honest...I'm no' being starved or beaten!

KATHY: Is it like what you expected?

IAN: The physical stuff *is* hard. You tell yourself it's going to be tough but it's only when you're soaked to the skin and totally knackered that you think 'what am I doing here?' But you do it...*and* the next time...and you think 'well I survived that'...sitting in an office would be warmer but a lot more boring!

THOMAS: *(Mouth full)* D'ye do that thing where –

KATHY: Don't speak with your –

IAN: *(Breaking in)* What's that wee man?

THOMAS: You know like in the pictures when they go under water through a drain and the guy's lungs are burstin' an...

IAN: Oh right.

JANIS: He means that 'Join the army' ad...'Take it to the limit'.

She shudders.

THOMAS: Dead scary.

IAN: No, they havnae made me do that but rivers, yes. We've had tae get across in full kit, the lot, and then double march across the moors soaking wet.

JANIS: What's the point?

IAN: Feels good when it's over.

ALLY: They're trainin' a fightin force...it's no just boy scouts with guns.

KATHY frowns a warning.

KATHY: And you're at college Sharon, is that right?

SHARON: Yes, sound engineering. I'm doing an HND just now but could transfer to uni if I decide to go for a degree.

IAN: She's a DJ at weekends!

JANIS: Brilliant. I wouldn't mind a course like that.

ALLY: You need to get decent grades in your subjects first.

JANIS: Give me a break.

ALLY: Sorry.

IAN: Thought we'd call in on Gran for an hour or so.

KATHY: It'll be nice for her to see you but you've only been here a few hours...

IAN: I thought tonight would be better...she's no' so great in the mornins. We don't need to rush off tomorrow. What shift you on, Ma?

KATHY: I don't start till twelve on Wednesdays.

IAN: Cool.

KATHY looks at ALLY.

SHARON: Is it okay for me to stay over?

KATHY and ALLY: *(Together)* Aye. Yes, of course.

SHARON: That's him again. He didn't say, did he? What's he like?

JANIS: Useless...but he's a bloke what d'ye expect?

IAN looks relieved; he's got away with it

IAN: I'll give Gran a bell. It'll only take ten minutes to drive over...that's if we can borrow the van?

ALLY: Aye, go on

IAN goes out to the hall to phone.

SHARON: *(Calling after IAN)* After we've cleared up.

KATHY: There's no need.

SHARON: I'll start washing. He can dry when he comes off the phone.

JANIS: I'll put away.

The girls go into the kitchen.

KATHY: See him! He was just chickening out of asking if they could stay over. Typical, leave it to the women to sort out. Yomp through bogs and rivers and cannae talk about anythin' that matters.

ALLY: Don't look at me...he wouldnae be yompin' anywhere if I had my way.

KATHY: Maybe but you're no exactly Mr Sensitivity either.

ALLY: Cannae win. Even Janis has got it in for me now. I see what you mean about her.

KATHY: It's her turn to get arsey, that's all.

ALLY: You're right...everyone's entitled to go off their folks. But naebdy tells you any of this do they?

KATHY: About bringin' up weans? No they don't.

She reaches out to touch his arm sympathetically.

IAN: *(Coming in with handset)* Gran wants a word, Dad

ALLY: Right. *(Takes handset from IAN and exits speaking)* Hullo mother, how ya doin'?

SHARON: *(From the kitchen)* Your dishtowel is waiting!

IAN: Yeah, yeah. *(Grins at his mother sheepish but enjoying the teasing)*

*KATHY pours herself more coffee listening to the banter
from the kitchen and ALLY'S voice from the hall. Relaxes.
ALLY returns.*

KATHY: How is she?

ALLY: Okay. She's all excited about Ian goin' over. (*Pause*)
Sharon's a nice lassie.

KATHY: Aye and she's got our Ian well sussed.

ALLY: She doesnae seem like the sort that would jist fall for the
uniform.

KATHY: Wonder if it's serious.

ALLY: Early days

KATHY: Talking of which...we'll need the sofa bed out. There's
only the single bed in his room.

ALLY: Aye. We can leave them to sort out who goes where.

KATHY: I suppose so. Thomas, have you done your homework?

THOMAS: I've no' much.

KATHY: Well it won't take long then...away and get it done.

THOMAS: Aw Mum, I'm watchin'...

ALLY: Well that's easy fixed.

Switches off.

THOMAS: Aw.

ALLY: Up the stair and no switching on up there!

*THOMAS goes. IAN, SHARON, and JANIS emerge from the
kitchen.*

IAN: All done Ma. We're off now...Okay?

JANIS: They're giving me a lift. I'll get my jacket.

IAN: Don't be hours doing your face.

JANIS makes a face at him and runs off.

SHARON: Thanks very much Mrs McLeod.

KATHY: Kathy!

SHARON: See you later then, Kathy.

ALLY: Glad to see you can keep that son of mine in order.

IAN: *(Good natured)* Shut up, Dad.

JANIS: *(Racing in with bag, scarf and struggling into jacket)* C'mon then!

ALLY and KATHY collapse into chairs laughing. Lights dim.

SCENE FOUR Kitchen Late morning next day

SHARON and IAN sit over the last of a late breakfast.

SHARON: Where is it your Mum works?

IAN: A sheltered housing place. She's an assistant manager. Sometimes has to sleep over nights.

SHARON: Right.

IAN: You should be at college, you wee skiver.

SHARON: I know, but I'll catch up. We don't have long.

IAN: Ah didn't know if you…well, you know.

SHARON: *(Smiling)* Know what?

IAN: We'd only just started seein' each other. You could have gone out wi' somebody else when I was away.

SHARON: Ah didn't.

IAN: I know.

SHARON: Oh do you now!

IAN: Don't be like that.

SHARON: It's okay, we're okay. Just…

IAN: Just?

SHARON: I don't like to think of you...in danger.

IAN: Like ma Dad says, it is the army. But I only have to do four years from I'm eighteen. Once I've got my trade....

SHARON: Mmm.

IAN: What?

SHARON: What if something happened...they could send you anywhere.

IAN: To a war zone, you mean?

SHARON: Yeah.

IAN: Things are okay just now.

SHARON: Yeah, 'just now'.

IAN: Sha-az.

He tries to distract her by cuddling.

SHARON: There's soldiers in different places...like peacekeeping forces...and it doesn't always look very peaceful.

IAN: Don't worry.

SHARON: Easy to say. *(Short silence)* See all that Queen and country stuff?

IAN: *(Cautious)* Yeah.

SHARON: D'you go for all that?

IAN: It depends what you mean. It's ma job but I'm no a big flag-waver. What's this about?

SHARON: Just getting to know you, that's all.

She ruffles his hair to lighten the mood.

IAN: Oh right.

The phone rings. IAN answers.

IAN: She's at work. This is Thomas' brother, can I take a message?...Oh...Ah see. D'you want me to come and get 'im then?...Okay, soon as.

He hangs up.

IAN: Thomas is no well. The school wants him taken home.

SHARON: Seemed okay last night. Did you see him this morning?

IAN: On his way out. Just said cheerio an that, didn't really notice how he was.

SHARON: Shall I come with you?

IAN: Would you? I'm sorry about this.

SHARON: What's to be sorry about? C'mon. Is it a taxi job?

IAN: We can start walking and pick one up on the way. Get him back here and see what's what.

Exit shrugging on jackets as they speak.

SCENE FIVE Living room Later

THOMAS on the sofa with a duvet round him. IAN on the phone to KATHY.

IAN: No, there's no need. I can wait here till you finish…She's here just now, just gettin' him a hot drink. She'll maybe get away in a bit…No, it's OK…Just seems shivery and says he's got a headache. The teacher said he didn't seem himself, worried or upset about something…he hasn't said anything, no…Aye here he is. *(To THOMAS)* Say 'hi' to Mum. Let her know you're not dead yet.

SHARON raises her eyebrows. THOMAS doesn't laugh.

THOMAS: 'Lo mum…uhhuh…mmm…I'm okay …yeah, she is…blackcurrant I think…Okay…see y'after. *(To IAN)* You're to go on again

IAN: Right Ma?…sure I will but I think he's okay. Probably just a fluey thing.

SHARON brings the drink.

SHARON: Did somethin' upset you? *(Pause)* Someone?

THOMAS shakes his head.

SHARON: You look tired. Did you sleep okay last night?

THOMAS mumbles.

SHARON: Sorry?

THOMAS: Bad dream.

SHARON: D'you often have them?

THOMAS: Sometimes

SHARON: Can you remember it?

THOMAS: No' really.

He shivers.

SHARON: Drink your juice. Not too hot?

THOMAS: *(Sips the drink)* It's fine... thanks.

SHARON: You're okay.

IAN has been watching this, his attention more on SHARON than on THOMAS.

IAN: You happy there pal or d'you want to go up to your bed?

THOMAS shakes his head

IAN: Stay down here? Okay.

Lights dim to blackout.

SCENE SIX Living room Late evening

KATHY and ALLY about to retire for the night.

KATHY: She better be in soon...it's ridiculous stayin' out this late on a weekday

ALLY: Well I'm not stayin' up...I'm knackered.

KATHY: Somebody's got to...she's no sixteen yet...and even if she was, what would you do? Go to sleep and ring the polis in the mornin' if she wisnae in 'er bed?

ALLY: God, Kathy, stop catastrophisin' and let's get our heads down. You'll hear 'er. You know what they say, 'Mothers don't sleep, they only worry with their eyes shut'.

KATHY is about to reply when they hear JANIS'S key in the lock. JANIS enters.

KATHY: What time d'ye think this is?

JANIS: I make it *(Consulting watch)* eleven forty four. Not waiting up for me are youse?

ALLY: That's enough.

KATHY: Well no actually we weren't. The world doesn't revolve around you in case you hadn't noticed.

JANIS: I'd worked that out...revolves round soldier boy doesn't it!

ALLY: Janis for God's sake. Your mother's tired and so am ah. We've only just got Thomas back down.

JANIS: *(Drops front, immediately concerned)* What's wrong wi' 'im?

KATHY: They sent him home from school...and he's had another of these nightmares if that's what they are. I don't know what's got into 'im...he gets in a real panic like he's runnin' a temperature an' seein' things.

JANIS: Has he seen the doctor?

KATHY: No yet...he seemed to brighten up when Ian and Sharon got him home. He was okay when he went up tae bed.

JANIS: Did he have his telly on?

KATHY: Ah don't think so. Why?

JANIS: *(Carefully)* Just wondered if maybe he'd seen somethin'.

ALLY: But he's had this before.

KATHY: No so bad tho'.

ALLY: Would it be them games on his Playstation?

JANIS: I doubt it...more likely to be the telly...he knows what's real and what's no' real.

KATHY: Are you saying he's watchin' stuff up there?

JANIS: We...ell,

ALLY: He's up there a lot...and he doesnae have that much homework.

JANIS: Ah didnae want to clipe on 'im.

KATHY: But...?

JANIS: He sometimes has it on late.

ALLY: Ah've no heard it on when we go up.

JANIS: You wouldnae.

ALLY: Whit d'ye mean?

JANIS: He wears his headphones doesn't he?

KATHY: Eh?

ALLY: His...where did he get them?

JANIS: He blagged them off someb'dy at school.

KATHY: I credited you with more sense. You're no a wean any more or that's what you want us to think. You might have thought of Thomas's good rather than jist sidin' wi' 'im for the sake of it! *(To ALLY)* He was mutterin' about burnin' and fire when I went up. Whit's he been fillin' his head with?

ALLY: Nae wonder he'll no say whit's buggin' 'im. He'll be scared of getting intae bother. *(Half admiring)* Fancy 'im getting' sorted wi' a headset.

KATHY: Aye well, it's no done 'im any good. But ye're right. We'll no' get a word out of him if we come on too heavy.

JANIS: Maybe he'll talk to me.

ALLY: *(Picking up the paper)* I'll check through the schedules.

JANIS: He might have borrowed a video.

KATHY: As if it's not hard enough keepin' 'im in line without you aidin' and abettin'.

JANIS: Ah never thought of it upsetting' 'im.

KATHY: You never thought...full stop!

ALLY: It's late...let's get tae wur beds. We'll see how he is in the mornin'. If he's okay for school, he should go. And we can speak to him tomorrow night.

Lights go down as they exit.

SCENE SEVEN Living room Next evening

KATHY sits on the couch with THOMAS, ALLY stands by the window.

KATHY: Thomas, we need to know what's buggin' you.

ALLY: You'll no get intae trouble son...was it somethin' you saw on the telly?

THOMAS: No really.

KATHY: You've had it on though when you should have been sleepin'?

THOMAS: Sometimes.

KATHY: Was there anything on that scared you? Anything horrible?

THOMAS is silent.

ALLY: *(To KATHY)* I checked. There was a documentary aboot Gulf War syndrome.

THOMAS: Is that the war in the desert? With the black head?

KATHY: The what?

THOMAS: *(Barely able to say it)* Sticking out the tank.

ALLY: Basra.

THOMAS: *(Remembering the images)* He was all black and burnt.

KATHY: What made you want to sit up and....

> ALLY restrains her.

ALLY: The man in the tank? Was that on the programme you watched?

> THOMAS nods.

THOMAS: It happened a while ago though? Before Ian joined the army?

> ALLY and KATH see the connection THOMAS is making.

ALLY: Aye son, that's a few years ago now.

THOMAS: But if there was a war, he'd have to go there?

ALLY: Not necessarily. It depends how many soldiers they need.

THOMAS: I don't want him to go. Make him not go Dad.

ALLY: He's a grown man now Thomas. I don't make his decisions for him, same as I won't make yours.

KATHY: The telly's coming out of your room, that's for starters.

THOMAS: Aw Mum.

KATHY: What's the point if it's keeping you awake and then giving you nightmares? And anyway, you've got your computer games, though I'm beginning to wonder if they're such a good idea.

THOMAS: That's different.

ALLY: Is it?

He and KATHY look at each other, unsure of what line to take.

Front door opens, SHARON and IAN enter living room.

IAN: Hi folks

KATHY: We weren't expecting to see you tonight.

ALLY: Come in. Sit down.

JANIS enters.

JANIS: Hi you guys!

SHARON: *(To THOMAS)* Hello you. How you doing?

THOMAS: Okay.

KATHY: He was back at school today. We were just having a wee chat...

ALLY: He'll be fine won't you son?

A silence falls.

KATHY: Everything okay?

IAN: Aye, it's just...I have to get back. My unit's been recalled.

KATHY: But you've only had half your leave!

IAN: I know but you can be ordered back any time.

KATHY: Well yeah but why...

He looks at ALLY. THOMAS becomes very still.

ALLY: Don't panic troops, war hasn't broken out or we'd have heard it on the news. They just can't get the mechanics these days...they need our Ian back!

JANIS: C'mon Thomas, let's raid the fridge, see if there's any Mars bar ice creams.

Both exit to kitchen.

SHARON: *(To THOMAS)* I like the sound of that.

Exits to kitchen.

IAN: The word is it's a peacekeeping tour...NATO.

ALLY: Bosnia?

IAN: Maybe. Bosnia, Kosovo. That's just the buzz.

ALLY: I suppose it's a possibility.

IAN: Don't look so worried. I'll be clearing roads and laying drains, probably. If we're being sent overseas, they're not going to whisk us away tomorrow.

KATHY: They'll tell you where you're going? I mean we'll get a forwarding address?

IAN: Sure, sure. It's not a top secret mission.

ALLY: (*Almost accusingly*) You're lookin' forward to it.

IAN: Aye, pity about the leave but, if it gets me to see a bit of the world..

ALLY: I just hope you like what you see.

KATHY: Don't start...

ALLY: I'm not. I meant what I said to Thomas. It was your decision and you have to make sense of it your own way.

KATHY: I don't know what to think.

The girls enter with THOMAS, who has an ice cream.

JANIS: So you're off in the morning?

IAN: First thing. (*To THOMAS*) Sorry wee man. That game of keepie-uppie will have to wait till next time. (*THOMAS manages a weak grin*) Don't you worry...I'll be back to annoy you all before you know it.

ALLY: I'll let your Gran know. Good job you went round to see her when you did.

There's a pause as they all digest the implication of this.

KATHY: Are you going back to Sharon's?

IAN: Aye, I've ma stuff to pack...and that.

He looks at Sharon.

KATHY: You'll no have long. Just the pair of you get away. Don't be a stranger Sharon. You just pop round whenever.

SHARON: Thanks. Janis has got my mobile number.

JANIS: We're gonnae have a night out.

IAN: (*Teasing*) Not sure I like the sound of that.

JANIS: Be afraid...by the time you get back, you'll have no secrets left!

ALLY: You've had it now!

Laughter. IAN gets up to leave.

KATHY: Give us a ring when you can.

IAN: Course I will Ma. Cheers, J.

He hugs JANIS and gives THOMAS a high five.

KATHY and ALLY exit with IAN and SHARON to the hall. JANIS left in the living room with THOMAS, puts her arm round him.

JANIS: He'll be fine Thomas. He'll be fine.

END OF PLAY

ACTIVITIES

Technique – Dramatic irony

In her introduction to *Between the Lines*, Alison Clark explains why she set the play in the year 2000, between the two Gulf Wars:

> I chose this because, in spite of Ian's optimistic point of view that there's no immediate crisis in the world, the situation is unstable enough to worry his family and his new girlfriend. The audience, of course, knows what the characters can't yet know – that the war in Iraq will begin in 2003.

She has used a technique called 'dramatic irony'. This is where a writer reveals or suggests something to the audience that the characters are unaware of.

Steps

Identify one or more examples of dramatic irony in *Between the Lines*.

Explain what you, the audience, knows but the characters don't.

Explain how this knowledge is given impact.

Evaluate the extent to which this knowledge adds to your understanding of the situation.

Mini essay

Your response to this task could be written as a 'mini essay' – a small section of analysis and evaluation with its own line of thought. A complete essay usually contains several sections like this which are used to justify the overall argument.

Suggested line of thought for mini-essay:

> Alison Clark's use of dramatic irony in the closing section of *Between the Lines* very effectively conveys the impact of war on ordinary families.

Critical essay

In the following essay, use *Between the Lines* as the play you write about.

> Choose a play which has a serious theme. With close reference to the play, show how the writer uses dramatic techniques to convey this theme.

Steps

In a group or on your own, identify the serious theme(s) and the dramatic techniques (for example, characterisation, theme, dialogue, climax) in the play.

Write your line of thought based on the question, plan the content of each section and write a topic sentence for each paragraph.

Write your essay.

Read your essay and score out anything that is not relevant to the line of thought.

Swap with someone else and give them a mark using the assessment criteria for your course. Give them 'two stars and a wish' feedback – two positive comments and one suggestion for improvement.

Structure
Your essay will be made up of several connected mini-essays which support the overall line of thought. Links between sections are shown.

Alison Clark's use of dramatic techniques in *Between the Lines* very effectively conveys the serious (theme of war.)

Humorous dialogue between the family members heightens the impact of the (theme by) offering a contrast to the (reality of war.)

Powerful imagery is used to bring the (reality of war home) (to the characters and) the audience (the black head).

The use of dramatic irony in the closing section very effectively conveys the (impact of war on ordinary families.)

Discussion

Thomas is traumatised by the images of a soldier who has been burned beyond recognition during the first Gulf War. (This refers to an actual photograph taken during the first Gulf War which was published by a few newspapers and self-censored by most.)

THOMAS: Is that the war in the desert? With the black head?
KATHY: The what?
THOMAS: (*Barely able to say it*) Sticking out the tank.
ALLY: Basra.
THOMAS: (*Remembering the images*) He was all black and burnt.

Use discussion of the following statements to help you identify useful areas for writing and talk assessments.

The media should protect the public from brutal images of war.
'– he knows what's real and what's no' real.'
Violent computer games are bad for children.
War is a necessary evil.
Three images that changed my life.

In Love

(a filmscript) by Iain Mills

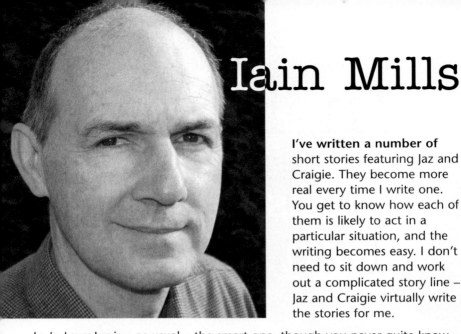

Iain Mills

I've written a number of short stories featuring Jaz and Craigie. They become more real every time I write one. You get to know how each of them is likely to act in a particular situation, and the writing becomes easy. I don't need to sit down and work out a complicated story line – Jaz and Craigie virtually write the stories for me.

In *In Love*, Jaz is – as usual – the smart one, though you never quite know how much of what happens is down to him.

The dialogue just wouldn't sound the same in Standard English. It's funnier in Scots, and sharper too. Most people I know speak Scots to a greater or lesser extent, so it makes sense to me to write in Scots. I also like to write about the kind of situations that can occur in anybody's life – drugs, bullying and death, but also fun, excitement and love. These themes are all around us. *In Love* looks at how drugs can affect people and relationships.

I don't see *In Love* as something written only for the stage. I see it more as something that would be recorded on DVD or video, filmed in real settings rather than on a stage. I'm sure if it's done that way, people will improvise – changing bits of dialogue here and there and perhaps adding some ideas of their own. I'm sure it will be all the better for it!

Iain Mills

About the author

Iain Mills writes for young people and adults in both English and Scots. He has had various short stories for young people published in anthologies such as *A Braw Brew* and *My Mum's a Punk*. His poems and short stories for adults have been published in anthologies and magazines including *New Writing Scotland* and *Rebel Inc.*

He lives in North Ayrshire and has worked in education as a teacher, university lecturer and education adviser.

SCENE ONE Outside Low wall Moonlight

CRAIGIE is sitting on a low wall. There are bushes behind him, and a large, exaggerated moon in the sky. He's holding a bunch of flowers and speaking to the camera.

CRAIGIE: See when Ah wis wee Ah used tae think aw yon 'love' stuff wis a loada rubbish, aw that haudin hauns an wee kisses in the moonlight an stuff. Ah widnae a believed Ah could be like that masel. *(Pause. Looks down.)* An then Ah met Ellen McGill...

SCENE TWO Street in post-war housing estate Dusk

A group of five boys are walking up the street, approaching a small row of local shops. They are carrying sports kit bags or poly bags (containing their football gear).

JAZ and CRAIGIE are together at the centre of the group. Some girls are hanging about outside the shops.

TAM MELVILLE: Ah'm goin in here tae get a drink...yiz comin'?

TAM, CRAIGIE & JAZ go into a newsagents shop; the others wait outside.

BOY 1: It wisnae thit they wur a better team, it wiz thit we wur aff form.

BOY 2: Ah juist thoat we wur rubbish an' they wur good.

BOY 1: That's whit ah saed.

GIRLS: *(Shouting at them)* Whit's in the bag? You goat yer pieces in ther?

BOY 1: Fitba gear, girls. Waant tae look?

GIRLS walk over to them.

TAM, CRAIGIE and JAZ come out of the shop swigging from their cans.

JAZ: *(Confidently)* Y'awright girls? Bet youse are glad we've arrived tae brighten up yer evening.

General banter, small-talk, slagging, giggling ensues. JAZ is at the centre of it, oozing charm. Camera zooms in on CRAIGIE, who has noticed a pretty blonde girl – ELLEN MCGILL. The other voices fade, replaced by exaggerated heartbeat noises as CRAIGIE stares at ELLEN. He tries to speak to her.

CRAIGIE: *(To ELLEN)* Eh...Ah've no' seen you around, eh, you don' school tae ma, eh, Ah mean, you don' go tae ma school, dae ye?

ELLEN: Naw, *(Laughs)* Ah go tae Heathcroft, Ah stay up that way...Ah'm jist down here tae see ma mates. Ah'm Ellen...whit's *your* name?

CRAIGIE: Aye. Whit? Oh, ma name...eh, Craigie. Ma Name's Craigie...Ah nearly forgot it ther. *(Laughs nervously)*

CRAIGIE: *(Voiceover as he stares at ELLEN)* God...whit's wrang wi me? Mibby Ah'm getting the flu. Ma mooths aw dry an sumdy's glued ma tongue tae the roof a ma mooth. In fact...it's no' even ma tongue...it's sumdy else's an it's twa sizes too big.

ELLEN: *(Glancing down at CRAIGIE'S sports bag)* So are you in the fitba team an aw, Craigie?

CRAIGIE: Me? Aye...star striker, that's me. Ye shoulda seen the wan Ah pit in the night...brilliant, so it wis. Ah'm hopin tae get a trial fur the District team...

ELLEN: *(Smiling at him)* Ur ye? That's brilliant Craigie...mibby Ah'll come an see ye play if ye get in the team?

CRAIGIE: Aye, that'd be... brilliant... *(Pauses as 'boy racer' car roars past)* See that motor...that's the kind Ah'm savin up fur... ma Uncle says he kin get us a part-time job...if he gets us it Ah'll be able tae afford wan nae bother...

ELLEN: Aye...they're brilliant motors, Craigie, wan ay ma brers has this really cool wee Ford, wi aw the spoilers an that.

ELLEN'S voice fades as CRAIGIE becomes aware of JAZ, behind ELLEN, giving him really strange looks and trying to get him to come over and speak to him.

CRAIGIE: *(As voiceover)* Whit's up wi him? *(JAZ is still making faces)* Whit's he wantin?

ELLEN: D'ye ever go doon tae Rooney's, Craigie? Ah think the music ther's brilliant.

CRAIGIE: Aye, sometimes... if Ah'm no' daein nuthin else, like... Sometimes me an Jaz...

JAZ: *(Going over to CRAIGIE)* Craigie...we'd better get goin. By the time we get doon the road, like... C'mon, let's make a move, eh? Ye comin? Right?

He stands waiting.

CRAIGIE: *(Looking irritated)* Right... O.K...*(Pause)* Jist geez a minute! *(Turns to ELLEN again)* Ellen...ye daein onythin the morra night?

ELLEN: Naw...nuthin special, Craigie.

CRAIGIE: Want tae meet us up the Wee Park then? Mibby aboot hauf seeven?

ELLEN: *(Enthusiastically)* Aye O.K. See ye there then.

JAZ grips CRAIGIE'S sleeve and practically drags him away.

CRAIGIE: *(To JAZ, annoyed)* Whit's aw that aboot? It's no' even hauf nine! Since when wur you ever in a hurry tae get hame? Whit's goin oan?

JAZ: 'V'yoo no heard a the McGill brers Craigie, Ellen's big brers? Cleaver an Banjo?

CRAIGIE: Well...ah mind the names...but whit aboot them? Whit've they tae dae wi me?

JAZ: Ther total heidcases, Craigie. Total bams. Drugs an aw yon stuff, an real vicious wi it. Ther supposed tae huv stabbt that wee guy McNulty...mind a him? Craigie...ye don' want onythin tae dae wi the McGills. Ye don' want tae go near *ony* a them. Ye'd better think aboot that afore ye go meetin Ellen McGill again.

SCENE THREE Low wall Moonlight

CRAIGIE: *(Speaking to camera, and still holding the flowers)* Ye ken aw yon stuff aboot 'love is blind' an aw that crap? It's true an aw. Ah could hear whit Jaz wis telling us an it aw made sense, sorta, but Ah kent Ah'd nae intention a takin his advice. Aw Ah could think of wis goin up ther tae see her again. Look, see when Ah'm telling ye aw this... *(Leans forward and lowers voice)* ... Ah'm gonnae miss oot a lot a the details, aw the kissin bits an stuff, an me an Ellen up the park an that... well, it's kinna embarrassin... An it's sorta... personal, like. Yiz widnae be interestit onyway, so Ah'll spare ye aw they bits. But we got oan real guid, me an Ellen. This wis aw new tae me. A lotta the time we jist talked aboot ordnary hings, like. Ah mind one time...innocent, like, askin her if she'd ony brers an sisters. 'Aye', she goes, 'Ah've twa big brers, James an Alastair', giein them ther Sunday names, like. Ah near says 'Whit wan's Cleaver an whit wan's Banjo?', but Ah stoapt masel in time. Ah goes 'Whit are they like?' an she goes 'Aw, ther great. See if sumdy messed us aboot like...', an she's looking at us kinna funny, an Ah feels this cauld shiver runnin up ma back, ken whit Ah mean? But Ah jist shrugs it aff an we... *(Raising hands in 'stop' gesture)* Naw...Ah says Ah wisnae gonnae tell yiz the personal bits. But how wis Jaz takin aw this?

SCENE FOUR Secondary school playground at break time

JAZ and CRAIGIE are talking in a corner of the school playground. JAZ is very serious.

JAZ: Ah wis talking tae big Tam Melville aboot they McGills. Ah'm telling ye Craigie, ther bad news.

CRAIGIE: Right Jaz, yiv tellt us that a hunner times, so ye huv.

JAZ: Naw, listen...ther no' jist usin aw sorta stuff, ther dealin an aw. You name it Craigie...the McGills'll sell ye it. An see if ye owe them an cannae pay...Tam says he kens a boy Banjo took a sword tae, whit a mess he wis Craigie....

CRAIGIE: Bit whit's that goat tae dae wi me, Jaz. It's no' Banjo Ah'm seein, is it?

JAZ: See that Ellen, Craigie? Ye want tae watch her. Ah mean, she kin seem nice an that, but...

CRAIGIE: *(Becoming angry)* Whit is it wi you, Jaz? *Ah* don' go oan an oan when *you're* seein a lassie, dae Ah? Ah mean... it's nane a your business, is it?

JAZ: Course it is Craigie...Ah mean, *sumdy's* goat tae look efter you if yiv no' the sense tae look efter yersel!

CRAIGIE: *(Pointing finger angrily towards JAZ'S chest)* Who dae ye think ye ur, talking tae *me* like that? Ye think yer that cool... Naebidy's supposed tae know onythin apart fae you. Sometimes Ah don' think yer hauf as smart as evrybidy thinks ye ur. Ah think yer jist...

JAZ: *(Interrupting by turning his back and starting to walk away, shouting back at CRAIGIE as he does so)* Onyway...yer no' gaun tae be much use tae the fitba team wi an airm hingin aff or yer kneecaps done in, ur ye!

SCENE FIVE Street near the local shops Daytime

CRAIGIE is walking down the street towards the shops. In the distance ELLEN is waiting for him. As he approaches her he's thinking out loud.

CRAIGIE: *(Voiceover)* Ah mean, Ah wis pure annoyed at Jaz, but Ah'm no' stupit...despite whit he thinks...an some a whit he said sunk in. Ah wis kinna wary at times but...

He reaches ELLEN. They smile radiantly at each other.

CRAIGIE: Hi Ellen...wher d'ye want tae go? D'ye want tae go doon the Sheepie?

ELLEN: *(Looking pleased with herself)* D'ye want tae come back tae *ma* hoose? It's jist ma brers that's in...

CRAIGIE hears JAZ'S voice – in voiceover – saying 'Careful Craigie man! Watch yersel'

CRAIGIE: Eh, eh, naw...Ah cannae. Ah cannae stay fur long...Ah'm supposed tae help ma faither wi his motor, he's expectin us back soon... Some other time mibby? 'Mon we'll jist sit oan the wa' here furra bit...

They sit down on a low wall near the shops. CRAIGIE turns to speak quietly to the camera.

CRAIGIE: Love's an amazing feelin but...

SCENE SIX Living room in Craigie's house Evening after dark

CRAIGIE is sitting in the living room casually watching TV. His mother – MAW – is doing the ironing at one end of the room. His DAD is sitting in an armchair reading the newspaper.

CRAIGIE: Maw, see when yer at the shops the morra, gonnae get us some a that shampoo...ye ken the wan Ah mean? The wan that stoaps ma heid itchin.

MAW: *(Smiling to herself)* Ah don' know whit's got into you these days Craig...yer aye washin yer hair these days. See if yer wee sister spent as long in the bathroom as you do, naebody would *ever* get in.

CRAIGIE: *(Defensively)* It's no' jist me. An ye used tae be aye complainin that Ah didnae wash masel, an see as soon as Ah dae...ye complain aboot that an aw. Ah cannae win!

MAW: *(Still smiling)* Yer costing us a fortune, son. Have ye ony idea a the price a that deodorant yiv got me buyin fur ye? D'ye know whit it costs? An whit ur ye wantin me tae get ye aftershave fur? If ye'd wan whisker on yer chin it wid be lonely...

DAD sits smirking to himself while pretending to read his newspaper.

CRAIGIE: *(Indignant)* Well Ah don' think it's fair getting oan at us jist because Ah'm tryin tae look smert. Ah don' complain when *you're* buyin perfume an that, dae Ah?

MAW: *(Laughing)* Okay, Craig! Keep yer hair on! Oh, Ah'm no' supposed tae mention yer hair, am Ah? Ye know, Craig, people'll think yiv a lassie hidden away somewhere.

CRAIGIE – blushing – gets up and stomps out of the room. As he goes, he shouts back at his parents.

CRAIGIE: That's no' ferr. Youse are aye pickin oan me. Ah'll jist go back tae bein dirty if it makes ye ony happier!

Slams door on way out.

DAD: *(To MAW, smiling)* Have you forgotten what it's like tae be in love? Ah think wee Craig's got it bad.

They laugh.

SCENE SEVEN Small park Dusk

CRAIGIE is arriving to meet ELLEN in a small swing park. She's sitting swinging on a swing while she waits for him. ELLEN is acting like a young child, and giggling strangely.

ELLEN: Whit's up wi *your* face, Craigie?

CRAIGIE: Nuthin. Jist ma Maw getting oan ma nerves. Ah cannae dae nuthin right.

ELLEN: *(Still clowning around on the swing and laughing)* Don' worry about it, Craigie. Don' worry aboot nuthin. *Ah* don' worry aboot things, dae Ah? Jist be happy, Craigie...like me, right? Ah've goat evrybidy looking efter us...you Craigie, an ma big brers. Alistair wis jist sayin tae me 'See if emdy ever gies ma wee sister ony hassle Ah'll cut them up intae wee strips a meat...that's if Ah don' jist kill them straight away...'

CRAIGIE: *(Looking at Ellen suspiciously)* You awright Ellen? Ye feelin O.K.?

ELLEN: Me? How would Ah no' be? Ah'm jist... Ah'm jist... Whit wis Ah gonnae say? Ah'm jist a bit dizzy Craigie. Ah think Ah'll go fur a wee sleep...

She walks away from him and goes over to a grassy patch and lies down on the ground. CRAIGIE walks over to stand beside her, looking concerned.

CRAIGIE: C'mon Ellen, ye cannae sleep ther. Whit's up?

ELLEN: *(Still lying on grass, smiling, eyes closed)* Nuthin... Nuthin... *(Quieter)* jist, nuthin.

CRAIGIE squats on the grass beside her, looking worried.

SCENE EIGHT Outside sports pavillion/Changing room Day

CRAIGIE and JAZ have just come out of the football changing room after a game, both carrying their football gear. As they walk along the road, CRAIGIE is speaking about the swing-park incident with ELLEN. He looks worried.

CRAIGIE: ...an she wis jist lyin ther... Ah didnae ken whit tae dae. At first Ah thought she wis steamin...but ther wisnae a smell a drink aff her or onythin... she wis totally aff her face but... *(CRAIGIE seems to be waiting for JAZ to say something, but he's keeping quiet)* Ah mean, wan minute she's oan the swings laughin an jokin an the next she's lyin oan the grass an wantin tae sleep. An why wid she say that aboot her big brers an cutting folk up? Ah mean, whit wis aw that aboot? *(JAZ is listening, but still doesn't respond)* Whit d'ye think, Jaz? Whit's up wi her?

As they walk on, JAZ just shrugs.

SCENE NINE Low wall Moonlight

CRAIGIE speaks to the camera. He's still holding the flowers.

CRAIGIE: But that wis really jist the stert. Efter that ther wis aw these rumours goin aboot, an Ah didnae ken whit tae think. Ah mean, how dae ye know whit's true an whit isnae? First ther wis the day Wee Grantie fae the fitba team came up tae us efter trainin. Ah mean...Wee Grantie's aff his heid but...

SCENE TEN Football changing room Daylight

The football team is just finishing getting changed after training. CRAIGIE is putting his gear into a bag when WEE GRANTIE comes over to him. GRANTIE is a small, spaced-out looking boy. He thrusts his face into CRAIGIE'S, and CRAIGIE has to back off slightly.

GRANTIE: Hey Craigie...Ah seen yon lassie a yours up the estate last night wi a boy. You no gaun oot wi her ony mair? Eh?

CRAIGIE ignores him, but GRANTIE persists.

GRANTIE: Ah mean, the twa a them wis awfy...

CRAIGIE: *Right* Grantie...Ah heard ye. Hey Tam...ye seen ma socks?

TAM: Zat them ower ther? Next tae the..

He's interrupted by GRANTIE.

GRANTIE: Ur ye listenin tae me Craigie? Ah wis sayin...

CRAIGIE: Ah ken whit ye were sayin, Grantie, an Ah'm no' listenin tae ye. Yer *aye* talking rubbish, so ye ur.

GRANTIE: But Craigie…*(CRAIGIE heads for the door, GRANTIE following him)* Craigie!

CRAIGIE exits, leaving GRANTIE standing.

SCENE ELEVEN School corridor Daytime

It's 'between classes' in the busy corridor of a secondary school. CRAIGIE and JAZ are walking along, almost side by side. CRAIGIE'S voice is heard in voiceover.

CRAIGIE: *(Voiceover)* An then ther wis that business wi Helen Scoular: Ah mean, Ah hardly even kent her…

A taller, slightly older girl, HELEN, pushes through the crowd to walk beside CRAIGIE. JAZ is just in front, but doesn't turn round.

HELEN: Hi Craigie.

CRAIGIE: *(Turns to HELEN, looking slightly puzzled)* Helen?

HELEN: Listen, Craigie, eh, Ah jist want tae warn ye. See that Ellen McGill?

CRAIGIE stops and turns to face her.

HELEN: Ah heard she's gaun oot wi sumdy else. Ye want tae watch that yin Craigie. Ye cannae trust her.

HELEN turns and walks away in the opposite direction, leaving CRAIGIE standing looking after her. He looks at JAZ, who is waiting for him a few yards away, but JAZ doesn't say anything.

SCENE TWELVE Living room in Craigie's house Daylight

It's early evening, and CRAIGIE is sitting on his own watching TV.

CRAIGIE: *(Voiceover)* An then ther wis that time she gave Jaz a message fur me...

The doorbell rings, and he goes to the front door to answer it. He opens the door and JAZ is there.

JAZ: Okay, man?

Walks in past CRAIGIE, heads for the living room – with CRAIGIE following – and sits down in an armchair.

JAZ: By the way, Ah bumped intae Ellen when Ah wis daein ma papers. She says she cannae make it fur seeven an could ye make in eight instead? At least Ah think it wis eight.

CRAIGIE: *(Looking slightly puzzled)* Did she say why?

JAZ: *(Apparently becoming engrossed in TV programme)* Nope.

CRAIGIE: Nae reason? Did she say onythin else?

JAZ: *(Appearing not to hear him at first, then answering)* Eh... Nope.

CRAIGIE: *(Voiceover)* An then when Ah went tae meet her...

SCENE THIRTEEN Street leading to the 'wee park' Daylight (early evening)

CRAIGIE is walking, alone, up the street towards the same 'wee park' mentioned earlier (where ELLEN lay down on the grass). Several girls – about his age – are hanging about at the swings. He enters the park, looks around him, checks his watch (eight o'clock) and waits. Eventually he goes over to the girls, who are watching him.

CRAIGIE: Any a youse seen Ellen McGill?

GIRL 1: Aye, she wis here till aboot hauf an oor ago.

GIRL 2: Ur you the guy that stood her up? She wis pure bealin so she wis... Ah widnae like tae be in *your* shoes...

CRAIGIE: But she sent us a message...?

CRAIGIE takes a few steps away from them and stands thinking.

SCENE FOURTEEN Low wall Moonlight

CRAIGIE is sitting on the same low wall as at the start. He's still holding the flowers. CRAIGIE speaks to the camera.

CRAIGIE: So... as ye kin see, things wurnae goin too well. Ah mean, we sortit oot the swing park thing...eventually. She tried tae tell us she'd never met Jaz that night, never mind giein him a message, but Ah didnae quite believe her. *Ah endit up takin the blame, jist tae keep the peace. But ther wis ither things an aw. Like the phone message Ah goat...*

SCENE FIFTEEN Hallway of Craigie's house Daytime

CRAIGIE has just come in the front door, and swings it shut behind him. He goes through the hall, throwing his jacket onto the stairs, and enters the living room. His parents are both there, watching the news on TV.

MAW: Hi Son...

CRAIGIE: Whit's fur tea Maw?

MAW: Why? Are ye gonnae stay here lang enough tae eat it fur wance?

DAD: Ye mindin that message fur him?

MAW: *(Teasing tone)* Oh aye, a lassie phoned fur ye. Soundit quite nice.

CRAIGIE: Who wis it?

MAW: Some lassie cried Ellen.

DAD: *(Teasing)* Ellen! Oooo-oooooo!

MAW: Ach, leave the boy alane you! She said tae tell ye she had tae stay in the night. Dae Ah ken who she is Son?

CRAIGIE ignores her, and sits deep in thought.

CRAIGIE: *(Voiceover)* That's kinna weird.... Ah mean, Ellen *never* phones us at hame... It doesnae make sense.

SCENE SIXTEEN Approaching
'The Sheepie' (park) Daylight (evening)

*CRAIGIE and JAZ are walking down the road towards the
Sheepie Park. CRAIGIE is bouncing a football*

CRAIGIE: *(Voiceover)* So Ah endit up jist gaun fur a gemme a fitba
that night instead...

*They meet various others, and a kickabout game of football
ensues – jackets for goalposts etc. After a while they all sit
down together on the grass for a break, and a bottle of Irn
Bru is passed around.*

ANDY: Did yiz hear aboot Banjo McGill?

TAM: Whit? Ye mean they burglaries?

ANDY: Naw. He done some guy wi a blade an the polis ur efter
him. The guy's in a bad way.

BILLY: Ma faither says ther neighbours is getting up a petition
tae get them moved, him an Cleaver's bin breakin intae
ther hooses. An see that lassie...

He shuts up suddenly and glances at CRAIGIE.

BILLY: Eh... that...eh, that wis some goal ye scored Jaz. The wan
fae the left...

JAZ is sitting very quietly and doesn't appear to be listening.

SCENE SEVENTEEN Low wall Moonlight

Same wall as at the start, and CRAIGIE is still holding the flowers.

CRAIGIE: *(Speaking to camera)* Ah kent somethin wis wrang, but Ah didnae want tae really admit it tae masel. Ah still hoped things wid work oot atween us... ye ken whit they say...'love is blind'. But aw these things that wur happenin had me aw mixed up...the phone message, yon business wi Helen Scoular, the message tae Jaz an that... Ah kent Ah had tae get it sortit oot, an Ah went tae meet her wan night determined tae find oot whit wis goin on. It didnae quite work oot like that but...

SCENE EIGHTEEN Street approaching local shops Daylight (early evening)

CRAIGIE is walking towards the local shops. Four girls are standing outside the shops, talking quite loudly to each other. However as CRAIGIE gets near their voices drop to whispers, and they glance surreptitiously at him. A girl leaves the group and walks over to CRAIGIE. It's MARGARET, one of ELLEN'S friends.

CRAIGIE: Hi Magret.

MARGARET: Hi Craigie...listen, that's fae Ellen.

She hands him a folded note. CRAIGIE unfolds the note and reads it. He looks shocked. He stands there, re-reading it.

MARGARET: Y'awright Craigie?

CRAIGIE: *(Totally distracted)* Eh... whit? ... Aye...

He slowly turns his back and walks away. As he goes down the street away from the shops he's still reading the note.

SCENE NINETEEN Craigie's bedroom Day

CRAIGIE is lying on his back on his bed. The note lies beside him. He's just staring at the ceiling. After a moment the doorbell rings faintly downstairs, and muffled voices can be heard.

MAW: *(Shouting from downstairs)* Craig! That's Jaz fur ye! He wants tae know if yer goin oot furra game a football?

CRAIGIE: *(Shouting back)* Naw! Tell him Ah'm no' feeling well.

MAW: *(Shouting)* But that's whit Ah tellt him yesterday... an the day before that an aw...

CRAIGIE: *(Shouting)* Leez alane! Ah don' feel like goin oot...
(He rolls over to lie face down)

SCENE TWENTY Low wall Moonlight

Same wall as before, and he's still got the flowers. CRAIGIE speaks to the camera.

CRAIGIE: Ah'm no' gonnae tell yiz whit wis in the note. It wis too kinna personal, but basically she wis goin oan aboot stories she'd heard aboot me goin oot wi another lassie. *Me!* She made it clear if Ah ever went near her again her big brers wid be efter me. It really hurt us... *(Pause)*

Ah've no' seen Ellen fur ages, like. Ah goat tellt Banjo wis in the jile, an the family wis movin. Ther wis a story that Ellen goat pit intae care, but Ah didnae ken how much ay it wis true. Jaz jist kept sayin 'yer better aff wi'oot her Craigie; ther's plenty mair lassies oot ther waitin fur ye'. *(Pause)*

But that sorta goat me thinking... Ah mean, Ah wunnert if Jaz had something tae dae with it aw...he kin be awfy fly. Ther wis a loat aboot me an Ellen splittin up that Ah jist didnae unnerstaun, an a coupla times Ah wunnert if it wis wan ay his plans... but, naw. Ah don' hink he wid dae that tae us...*(Pause)*

By the way, see if yer wunnerin aboot the flooers...ther fur ma Maw. Ah forgoat her birthday, so me an Jaz jist made a wee detour through the park tae get some. Jaz aye comes up wi the guid ideas...

END OF PLAY

ACTIVITIES

Language – Scots vs Standard English

The dialogue just wouldn't sound the same in Standard English. It's funnier in Scots, and sharper too.

1 Choose a scene from *In Love* and translate it into Standard English.

2 Discuss whether you agree with Iain Mills that 'it's funnier in Scots'. Justify your point of view and suggest what this reveals about your perception of both Scots and Standard English.

3 Discuss whether you think there are situations where only Standard English or a Scottish language or dialect should be used.

4 Identify positive and negative attitudes to Scottish dialects and languages. This could be based on personal experience or wider research.

Research

Research Scottish languages, Scottish dialects and Standard English. If you did not do the introductory research task at the start of this book do it before starting the assessment below.

Assessment

Your research could provide the basis for an essay, group discussion or presentation, depending on the course you are following.

> Scottish languages and dialects are increasingly redundant in a modern world.

Discuss your reaction to this statement and suggest how valid it is.

Assess yourself and others using the criteria for the course you are following. Give each other two stars and a wish feedback – two positive comments and one suggestion for improvement.

Media production

I don't see *In Love* as something written only for the stage. I see it more as something that would be recorded on DVD or video, filmed in real settings rather than on a stage. I'm sure if it's done that way, people will improvise – changing bits of dialogue here and there and perhaps adding some ideas of their own. I'm sure it will be all the better for it!

Iain Mills

Take the writer's advice – make *In Love: The Movie*. Feel free to make it your own and translate dialogue into your own dialect or language.

The brief

Adapt scenes from *In Love* into a 10-minute film aimed at 14- to 16-year-old Scottish males and females. Any local dialect or language can be used.

You'll manage this task best if you or your teacher has some knowledge of video production, although, as you can see from the internet, you don't have to be an expert to produce an interesting movie. It is best done as a group production.

Steps

Choose which scenes you want to film.

Produce a storyboard and/or a shooting script. You will have to identify:

- camera movement and angles
- lighting
- sound – music, sound effects, dialogue.

Plan your production:

- When?
- Where?
- Do we need permission/consent for anything?
- What roles and tasks need to be filled?

Shoot and edit your footage.

Clear a space in your bedroom for the Oscar.

Bairns An' Feels

by
Charles Barron

CHARACTERS

JACK, *a bully, self-centred and very self-confident*

NICKI, *sensible, sympathetic mature*

VAL, *naive, gentle, other-worldly*

LOU, *nosy, gossipy*

TAMS, *boyish, but vulnerable*

RUTH, *quick-witted, amusing*

MOUSE, *Jack's assistant-in-crime*

THE GANG, *of mixed ages and sexes, easily swayed*

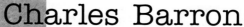

Charles Barron

About 30 years after my first production in 1957, I became aware of a growing interest in the dialect of my native Aberdeenshire, the Doric. It was now being studied in schools and writers were actually getting Doric prose and poetry published. It seemed appropriate to try my hand at putting it on stage since, like all dialects today, it is primarily a spoken medium. My first full-length Doric play, *Fooshion*, won the Mobil Oil Playwriting Award and that encouraged me to go on writing occasionally in the Doric, even though it meant that I was limiting my potential audience to the North East of Scotland since companies further south always claim that the dialect is incomprehensible.

There was something of a breakthrough, though, in 2005 when Learning + Teaching Scotland published *Amang the Craws* and put a copy into every secondary school in Scotland (though they did take the precaution of binding it with an English translation). As for *Bairns an' Feels*, I wrote it for a youth theatre in the North East to see how young people would cope with the dialect. It is in the kind of Aberdeenshire tongue spoken by most young people today – not nearly as broad as, say, rural grandparents speak amongst themselves, and as likely to draw on American idiom as on pure Doric. I don't think the dialect poses any problems for audiences; it is only in its written form that Doric is frightening.

It's a play about an outsider, one of the themes I return to again and again. Why is it that some children seem predisposed to be outside the group? Are they hurt by being excluded or is it, at least sometimes, the child's own choice? If so, why? Do outsider children grow up to be outsider adults, loners, misfits?

But that's all a bit solemn. The main purpose of the play is to provide some fun. What else is drama for? Fun above all for the participants, tackling roles that are not too far removed from their own lives but offer some kind of challenge; but fun too, I hope, for an audience afforded a glimpse into the sometimes alien minds of children.

Charles Barron

About the author

Charles Barron's first play was produced in 1957 while he was at University and his hundredth made it on to the stage in 2006. After University he taught (English, History, Latin, Greek) for four years, trained English teachers for seven and trained Drama teachers for 18. Then he became a part-time artistic director which gave him more freedom to write. Since 1998 he has been a full-time playwright. His plays have been mounted by professional companies, youth theatres and academic institutions, almost always in Scotland.

Most of his published work has been in the area of drama education – a string of study guides mostly on plays for Higher Drama, published by the Scottish Consultative Council on the Curriculum and by Learning + Teaching Scotland.

NOTES

Publisher's Note: There is a guide to the stage directions used in this play on page 174.

The scene represents an area of waste ground where children meet. There are things to sit on and others to hide behind – abandoned furniture and household equipment etc.

There are about a dozen children on stage. Some are perched high up on bits of rubbish. One child, VAL, is quite alone, far from the others. She is watching but not involved. She alone looks sad and withdrawn. All the others are excited. Most are clustered round TAMS, holding her by the arms and legs, giving her her birthday bumps. They are part way through as the curtain opens.

THE GANG: *(Bumping her)*
Five...six...seven...eight...nine...ten...eleven.

On the 'eleven' they swing her particularly high and drop her hard on the ground. All, including TAMS, laugh. She scrambles to her feet, breathless and excited.

TAMS: *(Happily)* Hey, 'at was sair! You're affa rough.

She rubs her bottom and they all laugh some more.

NIKKI: Happy birthday, Tams.

LOU: Here's your card.

She hands over a handmade card, not in an envelope. TAMS look at it, pleased.

TAMS: Is that supposed to be me on the front?

RUTH: Naebody else here has green hair.

Laughter. The drawing has green hair; TAMS hasn't.

TAMS: Aye, but I hinna got three eyes.

LOU: Fit did you get?

TAMS: Sandy's got it.

She gestures at her wee brother – or sister – one of the smaller children in the group. He/she is holding a small electronic game.

NICKI: You rescued it, did you, Sandy? When your sister was gettin' her bumps? 'At was good thinkin'! *(She takes it)* Oh, look. 'At's neat.

They all crowd round, making approving noises.

GIRL 1: I wish my Ma would gi'e me something like that.

GIRL 2: I bet it was dear.

RUTH: Na, she won it at the Bingo!

Laughter.

NICKI: Can you play it yet?

TAMS: I hinna had time to try. I was just lookin' at it when you eens grabbed me.

NICKI: Come on, then.

She gives the game to TAMS, who tries a few buttons.
They are all peering over her shoulder.

LOU: You're makin' him ging backwards.

NICKI: Try that button.

She demonstrates.

GIRL 3: No, that's nae richt.

She tries to press a button.

GIRL 4: Try 'at een.

She tries to reach a button.

GIRL 5: Dinna be feel.

LOU: Look, I'll show you.

TAMS: *(Moving away)* I canna see fit I'm daein' for you a'.

NICKI: Come on, noo, abody. Let her work it oot for hersel'.

THE GANG: *(All jostling in again)* No, I ken fit tae dee. I'll show her. She's got nae idea. Gi'e it to me. I've got een the same. *(Etc.)*

TAMS: *(Laughing)* Stop it. Get aff.

NICKI: You should have left it at hame.

TAMS: I ken. But I wanted you to see it.

RUTH: You wanted to show aff, you mean.

TAMS: *(Cheerfully)* Aye.

NICKI: Well, we'll leave you in peace tae get the hang o' it. *(To the Gang)* Won't we?

THE GANG: No!

NICKI: Oh, yes, we will.

> *She drives them all off, but Sandy makes a dive back to Tams's side.*

TAMS: You ana'. Especially you, you wee nuisance.

> *NICKI comes back, picks up SANDY exits.*

NICKI: Fit a weight you're gettin' tae be!

> *Left alone, TAMS climbs up on to an old fridge or something and settles down, intently playing her electronic game. Something goes wrong. She is annoyed.*

TAMS: Ach. 'It's happened again. I'll never get it oot.

> *She lays it down on her knee. Enter JACK, too self-confident, a swaggering bully.*

JACK: Is that your new een?

TAMS: *(Not keen to talk to him)* Aye.

JACK: Is it difficult?

TAMS: Aye.

JACK: *(Sneering)* Affa difficult?

TAMS: Nae too bad.

JACK: Gie's a shottie.

TAMS: *(Hastily lifting the machine)* No. I'm in the middle o' a game.

JACK: *(Nastily)* No, you're nae.

> *He grabs for the game but she manages to raise it out of his reach.*

TAMS: I am. Look.

She holds up the screen to him – but keeping it well out of his grasp.

JACK: So fit? I wint it.

He snatches it out of her hands, very roughly. She is frightened.

TAMS: Gi'e me 'at back. It's mine.

JACK: Nuh, it's mine noo.

TAMS: It's nae.

JACK: Aye, it is. Finders keepers.

TAMS: *(Near despair)* You didna find it. You stole it.

JACK: I didna. You gave it to me.

TAMS: I never.

JACK: You did.

TAMS: I didna. *(She wants to cry)* You grabbed it oot o' my han's.

JACK: Prove it.

TAMS: I dinna have to. It's my game.

JACK: *(Grinning, enjoying himself)* No, it's nae. You gave it to me, for a present, an' you canna ask it back. 'At widna be richt.

TAMS: *(Tears of frustration)* It's mine. You ken it is. It's mine. It's mine.

JACK: Ach, you're a richt bubbly-jock. You're aye greetin'.

TAMS: *(Through her tears)* I'm gan hame tae tell me ma. She'll be mad at you. She bocht me that for my birthday.

JACK: She'll be mad at you then, giein' awa' her birthday present to a loon you met in the street.

TAMS: *(Losing her temper, she springs at him)* Gi'e it back.

JACK: *(Easily throwing her off)* How d'you play this thing onywey? *(She is silent. He fiddles with it, unsuccessfully)* Tell me.

TAMS: No.

JACK: I'll brak' it if you dinna.

He raises it above his head, ready to throw.

TAMS: Dinna. Please dinna brak' it.

JACK: Show me hoo to work it, then.

Reluctantly, she comes to him and points out the controls.

TAMS: That button maks him rin an' that een maks him jump ower the gaps.

JACK: Fit gaps?

TAMS: Look.

She points at the screen. He tries a few button presses.

JACK: Fit's happened? It's gin blank.

TAMS: *(Not displeased)* You've lost a' your lifes. You're oot.

JACK: Fit wye div I start it again?

TAMS: I'm nae tellin' you. You've had your shottie, so gi'e it back to me.

JACK: *(Raising it)* Fit wye div I start it? *(Pause)* I'll smash it on the grun'.

TAMS: *(Scared again)* The green button. *(He does. He plays a few moments)* No, you've to mak' him jump ower the hole things or you loss a life every time he fa's in. *(He loses again)* See? You've lost again.

JACK: Ach, it's a feel game onywey.

Casually he smashes it to the ground. TAMS gives a little cry of despair and runs to pick it up. She takes it off to one side, nursing it.

TAMS: You've broken it, look. Completely.

JACK: Your ma'll need to buy you a new een, then.

TAMS: You will. You broke it.

JACK: Nae me. I never touched it. You must have broke it yoursel'. *(Nastily)* An' you canna prove different.

He saunters off. TAMS sinks down, crying again. The children enter from the other side.

NICKI: Weel, have you got on top o' that thing yet? *(Seeing her in tears)* Oh, Tams, fit's adee wi' you?

RUTH: Can you nae work it oot?

TAMS: Look. Look at my game. He's broken it.

Crowd react.

LOU: O' no. Fa did 'at?

TAMS: Yon coorse loon, Jack.

NICKI: Him! Fit were you thinkin' o', lettin' him play wi't?

TAMS: I couldna help it. He took it aff me.

LOU: He would.

RUTH: Fit a nerve.

NICKI: Do you think it can be sortit?

TAMS: No. Listen. *(She shakes it and the others can hear that everything is loose inside)* An' the screen's a' smashed, look.

Crowd reaction. One of them takes it from her for a closer look.

NICKI: You should tell the teacher.

TAMS: He'll just deny it. He'll say I dropped it or something.

LOU: Richt enough. He's affa ill-tricket.

NICKI: It's time something was deen aboot him.

TINY CHILD: I could bash him for you.

NICKI: Good for you. But I dinna think there's enough o' us to haud him doon for you.

RUTH: We canna bash him, but there's maybe enough o' us to persuade him to pay for the damage.

THE GANG: Aye. Let's dae it. Come on and find him. *(Etc.)*

NICKI: A' richt. But leave the speakin' to me. *(She points warningly at the TINY CHILD)* An' mine, noo, you...nae violence.

Cheers and shouts as they all go charging off to find JACK. All, except VAL, who hangs back, shy and quiet. The games machine has been left lying by the child who had it last. VAL goes to it and comes downstage with it. She strokes it gently, holds it to her ear, and then strokes it again, ritually. JACK appears at the back of the stage, watching. She doesn't notice him.

She again raises the machine to her ear, listens, nods solemnly and tries out the buttons. It is clearly working again. JACK comes forward.

JACK: Let me see 'at. *(He grabs it from her. VAL shrinks away from him. He tries it out)* It's working. But it was a' smashed up. Fit have you deen tull't?

VAL: *(Gently. There is an other-worldly, elfin quality about her)* It's all right now.

JACK: *(Aggressively)* You fixed it? *(Val nods)* Hoo d'you manage 'at? *(Val shrugs)* Hiv you deen't afore? *(Val nods)* You can mend things?

VAL: *(Sadly)*: Not people. And not animals. Just...things.

JACK: Honest? *(She nods. He is torn between hope and disbelief)* Na, it's nae possible. *(She shrugs again, not caring whether he believes or not)* Prove it then. *(Pause. She just looks at him, expressionless)* A' richt, I'll find something.

He dives into the rubbish and finds a broken old radio. He tries switching it off and on to prove that it is dead.

JACK: Could you sort this?

She takes it, without expression. She strokes it in the same kind of way and then hands it back to him. Suspiciously he switches it on; a blare of music. He is flabbergasted – and delighted. She shows nothing.

JACK: Hey, 'at's great 'at. Hiv' you aye been able to dee it?
(*She nods*) Are you famous for it? (*She shrugs*) Dis onybody
ken aboot it? (*She shakes her head. He starts to get ideas*)
Well, dinna tell onybody, a' right? (*She says nothing*)
Div you hear me? Dinna tell onybody fit you can dee.
(*She stares at him*) If you div, I'll batter you. (*She stares.
He is getting angry*) Are you listening to me? (*Nothing.
They hold a stare*)

VOICE (*Off*): There he is.

ANOTHER VOICE: Come on, abody.

*THE GANG rushes back in but don't come too close to JACK.
VAL turns silently away.*

NICKI: We've been looking for you.

JACK: Oh? Fit for?

NICKI: (*Indicating TAMS*) You broke her game.

JACK: Fit if I did?

NICKI: Well, we want you to pay for it.

JACK: (*Nastily*) Div you, now?

NICKI: Aye.

THE GANG: Aye! We div. You have to dee it. (*Etc.*)

JACK: And fa's gan tae mak' me?

TINY CHILD: (*Fists up*) I will.

NICKI: (*Putting the tiny child behind her*) We a' will.

*JACK looks round. There is a hostile circle around him.
He decides to play it safe.*

JACK: Well, let me tell you, that you're a' jist wastin' your time.

*NICKI steps forward threateningly. There is a similar
movement by everyone.*

NICKI: Oh, are we?

JACK: Aye, you are, because...there's nothing wrang wi' her
stupid machine.

He hands it to NICKI who tries it out, wonderingly.

JACK: See?

NICKI: 'At's funny. It's working.

LOU: But it's insides was a' oot o' ither. I could hear them rattling aboot.

NICKI shakes it to her ear, shrugs, hands it to LOU who shakes it.

LOU: Nae rattle noo. *(She tries it)* And it's definitely working. Look, Tams.

She hands it to TAMS who also tries it out.

NICKI: *(To JACK)* So you've been lucky this time. But jist dinna let me catch you interfering wi' onybody's things again. Okay?

JACK: I never did onything.

He walks away.

LOU: You should tak' it hame, now, Tams, and keep it safe.

TAMS: I will. This is really lucky, isn't it? I thought my machine was completely useless.

She is intent on a game already. LOU guides her off.

RUTH: *(To NICKI)* I dinna understand this. I saw that thing an' the screen was just in smithereens.

NICKI: I ken. But it looks a' richt noo.

GIRL 1: Maybe it's nae the same machine?

NICKI: You mean Jack went an' got anither een to replace Tams's?

GIRL 1: It would explain why it was working now.

RUTH: Especially the screen. In fact, it's the only explanation for the screen.

NICKI: *(Puzzled and worried)* It doesna seem like Jack to dee something like that.

RUTH: An' far would he get anither een the same?

NICKI: Weel, since it's Jack we're speakin' aboot, there canna be onything good behind it.

RUTH: Do you think it fell aff the back o' a larry?

NICKI: I wouldna be surprised.

> *Everyone drifts off, except VAL who sits down in her usual lonely, sad state.*
>
> *Pause.*
>
> *Enter JACK, carrying a video machine. He lays it down in front of VAL. She looks up at him.*

JACK: Mend it.

VAL: What's wrong with it?

JACK: It doesna work.

VAL: Is it yours?

JACK: Aye. I've had it for years but it got broken.

VAL: *(Shrugging)* All right.

> *JACK puts it on her knees and she does her usual stroking.*
>
> *Enter two young girls: GIRL 6 and GIRL 7. They watch as VAL hands it back to JACK and goes off. He notices them.*

JACK: Aye, aye.

GIRLS: *(Together)* Hello.

JACK: Nice, is it?

GIRL 6: It's a' richt.

JACK: Have you got een?

GIRL 7: We've got een at hame, aye.

JACK: But have you got een o' your ain? In your ain bedroom?

GIRL 7: No-o-o.

JACK: Would you like een?

GIRL 6: *(Suspiciously)* Fit wye are you askin'?

JACK: 'Cos I could let you ha'e this een, if you like.

GIRL 7: Is it yours?

JACK: Aye. *(Pause)* But I'm sellin' it.

GIRL 7: How much?

JACK: Twenty pounds. It's a real bargain.

GIRL 6: Are you sure it's yours?

JACK: Of course it's mine.

GIRL 7: Fit was that ither girl daein' wi' it?

JACK: She was thinkin' o' buyin' it. But I'd raither sell it to you.

GIRL 7: Fit wye?

JACK: I dinna like her.

GIRL 6: *(Doubtfully)* I'd ha'e tae ask my Da.

JACK: 'At's Okay.

GIRL 7: And mak' sure it's workin'.

JACK: *(Confidently)* This video works a treat.

GIRL 6: A' richt. Come hame wi' me an' ask my Da.

JACK: *(Delighted)*: He'll tell you. It's a real bargain.

> They all go off.

Mime Sequence One

Fast music begins. Lights flash and then settle to five tight spots around the stage. During the next sequence everything moves very fast, like a silent movie. VAL steps into the USC spot; a girl appears in each of the other four. They may include some of the named characters – it doesn't matter.

JACK trots to GIRL A; she hands him a broken watch; he trots to VAL who does the business on it; he returns it to GIRL A; she unlocks a cash box and pays him for the repair. He pockets the money carefully.

He crosses to GIRL B, she offers him a TV; he pays her a £1 coin for it; a tough-looking girl, MOUSE, appears and helps him carry it to VAL for repair; then to GIRL C who gives them a pile of notes for it. JACK pockets the cash, after giving his assistant a single note.

They go to GIRL D who offers to sell him a clock. He shakes his head over it and tosses it away; she shrugs and leaves; he retrieves it, takes it to VAL for treatment and then takes it to GIRL A, who again unlocks her cash box and produces some notes with which she pays him for it. MOUSE accompanies him.

The lights come back up; Girls A, B and C leave; the music ends. JACK is left alone with his assistant.

JACK: Hoo much hiv we made this week?

MOUSE: Nearly £100. Good, eh?

JACK: *(Dissatisfied)* Chicken-feed, 'at's a', jist chicken-feed.

MOUSE: Fit div you mean?

JACK: Did you see hoo much money that quine had in her cash-box?

MOUSE: *(Eyes glowing)* Oh, aye.

JACK: A lot mair than £100.

MOUSE: Oh, aye.

JACK: It would be rare to get some o' that, eh?

MOUSE: Oh, aye.

JACK: So ging an' get it.

MOUSE: Oh, aye. *(Starts to go; does double-take, returns)* Fit?

JACK: Get it.

MOUSE: Me?

JACK: Aye.

MOUSE: Fit if I get caught?

JACK: You winna.

MOUSE: They'll come lookin' for us as seen as they notice the box has disappeared.

JACK: They'll never notice.

MOUSE: Fit?

JACK: Listen. You sneak into the hoose, get the box and bring it here. I'll tak' oot some money...jist some o' it, nae it a'...an' you'll pit it back. Naebody'll be ony the wiser.

MOUSE: But it's locked.

JACK: I can...get it open.

MOUSE: Fit wye?

JACK: Never you min'. It's neen o' your business. Jist leave it to me. Noo, aff you go.

MOUSE: *(Wrestling with her conscience)* I dinna ken.

JACK: *(Nastily)* Get it...unless you want big trouble.

He moves towards her threateningly. She goes – fast. He grins and then assumes his 'nice' voice.

JACK: Va-a-al. Are you there?

VAL enters, quietly. JACK speaks jovially.

JACK: Hi, Val. Foo are you doin'?

She shrugs.

JACK: I've got a present for you.

She waits. He brings out a couple of £1 notes and offers them to her.

JACK: Here.

VAL: Why?

JACK: Jist a present. You've been deein' a lot tae help me lately. So I thocht I'd gi'e you something.

VAL: *(Shaking her head)* No, thank you.

JACK: You deserve it. You've saved me a lot o' money 'is last wee while, mending a' my broken things.

VAL: *(Naively)* A lot of your things seem to get broken.

JACK: I'm just unlucky, I suppose. *(Smarmy)* Except that I'm affa lucky, ha'ein' a frien' like you to fix 'em. *(He flutters the notes in her direction, but she shakes her head and turns away)* In fact, there is another wee job I was hoping you would do for me. *(VAL turns back to face him)* It's my...er...stamp collection.

Pause. VAL waits.

JACK: I've got a big stamp collection, you see. An' my Da gave me a...kind o' a box thing to keep them in.

Pause. She waits.

JACK: But I've lost the key. *(He laughs, unconvincingly)* Feel, eh?

Pause. No reaction from her.

JACK: So, I wondered, like, if you would min', jist opening it for me?

Pause. She shrugs.

JACK: 'Cos I'm affa missin' my stamps, ye ken. I ha'ena seen them for ages.

Pause. She looks.

JACK: So, 'at's a' richt, then?

Pause.

JACK: You'll dee that for me?

> *Pause. She nods. He shows relief. MOUSE comes racing in, looking anxious. She carries the cash box.*

MOUSE: Here it is, Jack. Here's your cash box.

JACK: Stamp box.

MOUSE: Stamp box?

JACK: *(Firmly)* Stamp box.

MOUSE: *(Puzzled, but agreeing)* Stamp box.

JACK: *(Pleased)* Stamp box. *(Taking it)* Turn your back.

MOUSE: Fit?

JACK: I dinna want you to see.

MOUSE: See fit?

JACK: *(Nastily)* Dee fit you're tellt.

> *She turns away. JACK smiles to VAL and holds out the box, persuasively. She does her stroking bit. He checks that the box opens.*

JACK: Thank you, Val. I winna keep you hinging aboot here ony langer. You dinna want tae be bored wi' me coontin' my stamps, div you?

> *VAL shrugs and goes.*

JACK: Richt, haud this.

> *MOUSE turns and holds the box while JACK takes out piles of money. He stuffs about half of it into his pocket and puts the rest back. Then he has second thoughts, opens it up again and takes some more out. Then he slams the box shut, and checks that it has locked.*

JACK: Pit it back.

MOUSE: I'm feart.

JACK: *(Pleasantly)* Fit are you feart o'?

MOUSE: Gettin' catchet.

JACK: *(Smiling gently)* Of course you're feart o' gettin' catchet. *(Nastily)* But you're mair feart o' annoyin' me.

MOUSE: Oh, aye.

She turns and runs. Music and lights for another 'silent movie' sequence.

Mime Sequence Two

MOUSE trots towards USR, meets Girl A, turns and runs to USL, meets Girl B, turns and runs to DSR, meets Girl C, turns and runs off DSL. The three girls chase her; they re-appear USL and chase across to USR; re-enter DSR and cross to exit USL; re-enter DSL and run to down centre where the MOUSE runs straight into Girl D. She is grabbed and the box taken from her. Girl A opens it with her key, shows horror. All point accusingly at MOUSE. The whole cast enter. Music stops. Lights back to normal. They have arranged themselves like a court, with NICKI in charge. MOUSE is held by a couple of girls. JACK is keeping well back. VAL, too, is almost out of the group, but not near JACK.

NICKI: I'm surprised at you, Moose. Jist fit div you think you're daein'...stealin' Jenny's money?

MOUSE: I never. It wisna me. Look.

She pulls out her pockets to show they are empty.

NICKI: We found you wi' the box.

RUTH: And there's a lot o' money missin'.

NICKI: So far is it?

MOUSE is anxious and scared – but self-preservation wins.

MOUSE: He's got it.

She points at JACK. They all turn and look at him. He turns to run but THE GANG block his way. He stops, resigned.

NICKI: Noo, that maks sense. *(To MOUSE)* Did he threaten you?

MOUSE: *(Eagerly)* Oh, aye.

LOU: You've done it this time, Jack. I'm gettin' the police.

THE GANG: Aye. That's fit tae dee. Go on, Lou. He's been askin' for it. *(Etc.)*

JACK: Jist a minutie.

Pause. They are uneasy – but not inclined to ignore the threat in his voice.

JACK: You'd better listen tae fit I've got to tell you.

He strolls confidently to centre stage.

NICKI: You're nae gan tae argue your wye oot o' this, Jack.

JACK: *(In an innocent, anxious-to-please voice)* I'm nae arguin'. I took the money a' richt.

Crowd reaction.

JACK: And I've done a lot o' ither wicked things 'is last few weeks.

Crowd reaction.

JACK: I sellt *you* a video.

The video buyer nods, puzzled.

JACK: But it wisna mine to sell. Nor was your walkman, or your TV. An' I didna mend your watch, even though I charged you for deein' it. No, neen o' that was me. It was a' deen by her.

He points. Everyone looks at VAL, who shows no emotion.

NICKI: Val? Dinna be ridiculous. She never pits a fit wrang. She's ower feart.

JACK: You dinna ken her. I think she's some kind o' a witch.

NICKI: Oh, Jack!

JACK: No, seriously. She mended a' that stuff. Min' thon game? You couldna understan' hoo I managed to sort it? Weel, I didna. It was her.

NICKI: I dinna believe you.

JACK: *(Totally confident)* Ask her.

Pause. NICKI isn't sure. JACK is very convincing. The others exchange wondering looks.

JACK: Hey, Val. Come ower here.

She comes.

JACK: You can mend things, can you?

Pause. Then she gives a single brief nod.

JACK: See? Fit did I tell you?

NICKI: You mended Tams's machine?

VAL nods.

NICKI: And the video machine?

Val nods.

NICKI: And the tv?

VAL nods.

NICKI: How do you dee it?

VAL shrugs.

NICKI: Well, I just dinna ken fit to think.

RUTH: Can you prove it? Show us?

VAL nods.

RUTH: Has onybody got something that doesna work?

Crowd discuss this loudly.

THE GANG: I hinna got onything. I wouldna gi'e her onything o' mine. She micht steal it. I wouldna trust her. *(Etc.)*

NICKI: Be quiet, a' o' you. We have to find oot the truth. Look for something.

They all look through the pile of rubbish, loudly rejecting anything the others find.

RUTH: This'll dee. This is a good test. *(Crowd reaction as she raises an abandoned old mantlepiece clock)* A' richt, Val. Dee your stuff.

VAL does her usual calm stroking. Pause. It starts to tick and then it chimes. Huge crowd reaction.

NICKI: I dinna believe my ain een. Or my ears!

LOU: Val, did you open the cash box?

VAL nods.

LOU: 'At's it, then. *(To NICKI)* She's the crook.

Crowd murmur against VAL.

JACK: *(Sure he has won)* Fit did I tell you?

NICKI: *(To Jack)* Ah, bit you're nae aff the hook yet, Jack. It was you that was selling the things. And Moose says you've got the money oot o' the box.

JACK: I tellt you. She's a witch. She made me dee it. She...bewitched me.

Big reaction from the gang.

THE GANG: Oooooh.

JACK: *(Big act, hand to forehead)* In fact, tae tell the truth, I can hardly min' fit it was she made me dee. It's a' a kind o' haze. Like I was hypnotised.

Reaction from crowd.

LOU: *(To VAL, bitterly)* I used to like you.

Music and lights for another mime sequence.

Mime Sequence Three

The entire cast move into a big semi-circle round the back of the stage. VAL moves first to LOU. As she approaches, LOU very deliberately turns her back. VAL then moves to RUTH, who turns away. She moves to a couple of others; not only they but the few children on either side of them turn away until only NICKI is left. VAL approaches her. Pause. NICKI turns away, too. Sadly, VAL walks off-stage. Music stops. Lights come up to normal. The others start to walk off, talking amongst themselves.

RUTH: I just wouldna've believed it o' her.

LOU: I ken. Maybe Jack's richt, an' she is a witch.

TAMS: Do you think we should tell the police?

NICKI: I suppose so. There's nae kennin' fit she micht dee next.

LOU: It maks you feel funny, just thinking' aboot that clock. An' her hands, the wye she touched it. That was real creepy, was it?

They have all gone, except JACK, forgotten by all of them except for the TINY CHILD who earlier threatened to beat him up. The child approaches JACK.

TINY CHILD: I could've deen it, ye ken.

JACK: Fit?

TINY CHILD: I could have beaten you up, thon time, easy. But they widna let me.

JACK: *(Nastily, not jokingly)* You? You couldna beat up a flee.

The TINY CHILD makes a dive at JACK, fists swinging. Contemptuously JACK picks the child up, pops her into an abandoned freezer or cupboard and bangs the lid shut. The child screams. JACK grins and saunters off, cock of the walk. Some of the older children hurry back in, drawn by the scream.

NICKI: Fit was that?

TAMS: It sounded like somebody screaming.

RUTH: 'At's fit I thought.

> *There is a wee scream from inside the freezer. They run to it.*
> *Everyone else comes back in – with JACK keeping to the edges*
> *and VAL hidden by the crowd. RUTH knocks on the freezer.*

RUTH: Hello? Fa's in there?

LITTLE CHILD: *(Voice off)* Me!

NICKI: Fa's voice is that? *(Louder)* Can you hear me? Fit's your name?

LITTLE CHILD: *(Voice off)* Lindsay.

NICKI: The poor wee soul. Help me, Ruth. Get it open. *(She, RUTH and LOU struggle with it)* She must have climbed in an' the lid banged shut on her.

RUTH: It's locked.

LOU: It canna be.

NICKI: *(Struggling with it)* It is. It's fa'en ower when the lid banged.

> *She's getting anxious, the only one mature enough to*
> *appreciate the real danger.*

NICKI: Ruth, run to the phone. Dial 999. *(RUTH is running already. She shouts after her as she disappears)* The Fire Brigade, that's fit we want. I hope they're quick.

LOU: The quinie'll be a' richt. *(Shouting)* Dinna be feart. We'll ha'e you oot in nae time.

NICKI: I dinna ken if there's much air in there. We maybe hinna got much time.

> *Crowd react. They are all beginning to panic. VAL makes her*
> *way quietly through the crowd and approaches NICKI.*
> *The crowd give her nasty looks and keep away from her.*

VAL: I can do it.

*NICKI looks at her for a moment and then steps aside. There
is no sign of gratitude on anyone's part. VAL strokes the lock.
Then she pulls it open. Immediately NICKI and LOU leap in to
lift the lid, the crowd cheer, LITTLE CHILD/LINDSAY is helped
out and everyone tries to hug her at once. RUTH dashes in.*

RUTH: The phone's broken. I'll ha'e to try the ither een.
(She stops as she sees the lid open and LITTLE CHILD/LINDSAY safe)
Oh. You've done it. 'At's great. How did you manage?

*Silence. Everyone looks at VAL. Pause. VAL looks at them but
there is no smile, no gratitude on any of their faces, just
suspicion and distrust. She turns and walks slowly off-stage.
NICKI takes a step or two after her, as if to call her back – but
she changes her mind. She turns back. VAL goes off. RUTH is
hugging LITTLE CHILD/LINDSAY. Everyone starts talking at
once, happy and hysterical, looking at LITTLE CHILD/LINDSAY.
Music swells up to drown them out. Slow fade to black out as
the curtains close.*

END OF PLAY

ACTIVITIES

Script adaptation – Mime Sequence One

You are going to adapt Mime Sequence One. It will help if you work with others.

The Rules

Include everything from the mime sequence.

Dialogue, stage directions and layout should be in the same style as the rest of the play.

The Plot

Summarise what happens in this sequence.

Suggest what you think the audience will learn or realise after watching it.

Summary advice

Before you write a summary, list all significant incidents/actions. Narrow this list down further by crossing out any items you don't need to refer to to make the action clear.

Characters

List all the characters named in this sequence.

They may include some of the named characters – it doesn't matter.

Note that the direction here is deliberately vague to allow flexibility when directing; decide which characters you will include and justify their inclusion.

Write a brief character sketch of each character you are using based on the rest of the play: their characteristics; the way they speak; the way they move; their motivation; the way they are lit, dressed, made up.

Find quotations from the text which could be used to justify your statements about the characters.

Theme

Identify the theme(s) of *Bairns An' Feels* and then write a 'mini-essay' which explains how this scene contributes to your understanding of the theme.

Suggested line of thought:

> In Mime Sequence One dramatic techniques are cleverly used to highlight the theme of exploitation by showing how Val's gift leads to her being both used and rejected by others.

Dialogue

Suggest what the characters might be saying to each other as they exchange money and goods. Then plan what is said, when it is said and how it is said.

Preparing to write the Doric script

If you are not a Doric user do some research to make your dialogue sound real by:

- compiling a dictionary of the Doric vocabulary and phrases used in *Bairns An' Feels*.

- searching the internet for relevant sites, particularly those with audio or video of Doric speakers.

- watching episodes of *River City* which feature some of the few Doric speaking characters on television, to get a feel for how it sounds.

- write the sequence first in your own language or dialect then translate it.

Stage directions

List all *actions* carried out by characters, for example, 'JACK *trots to* GIRL A' and list all *directions* about staging, for example '*Lights flash and then settle…*'

Note features of the style of Charles Barron's stage directions and make any changes needed to make your stage directions fit in with those used in the rest of the play.

Finally, write your Doric scene.

Performance

Rehearse and perform your scene in your best Doric.

The Snob Cross Incident

by
Moira Burgess

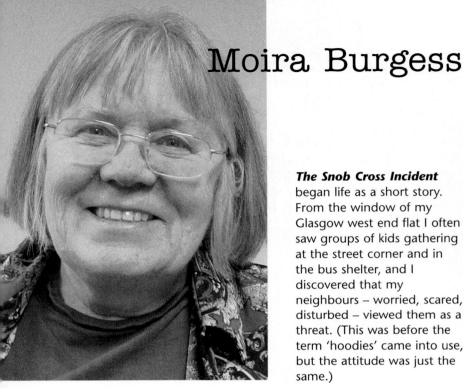

Moira Burgess

The Snob Cross Incident began life as a short story. From the window of my Glasgow west end flat I often saw groups of kids gathering at the street corner and in the bus shelter, and I discovered that my neighbours – worried, scared, disturbed – viewed them as a threat. (This was before the term 'hoodies' came into use, but the attitude was just the same.)

Since my children were much the same age, the kids didn't seem threatening to me, and I started thinking about the situation from their point of view. When I came to write the story, it seemed to work best from the viewpoint of one of the frightened neighbours, but I tried to make it clear that she was locked in her own fears and prejudices, unwilling to try to understand the kids. The story was written in the form of the frightened woman's diary – in other words, more like speech than formal prose – and so it went very easily into the shape of a play. Of course it can still be read, but I would hope it might sometimes be acted, and I've tried to make sure that it can be produced with the minimum of scenery and props, in a classroom for instance. I think school-age performers will know what I'm talking about in *The Snob Cross Incident*, and I hope any 'neighbours' in the audience will begin to understand too.

Moira Burgess

About the author
Moira Burgess was born in Campbeltown, Argyll, and now lives in Glasgow. Writing has been the most important part of her life since childhood and she has published two novels, *The Day Before Tomorrow* (1971) and *A Rumour of Strangers* (1987), as well as short stories, a play and the occasional poem, and many articles on a variety of topics. For some years she produced mainly non-fiction, including a book about Glasgow novels, *Imagine a City* (1998). Her current interest is the Scottish author Naomi Mitchison and she is working on a book about her. Like most writers, Moira has spent a lot of time going round giving talks to writers' groups and conferences, but more or less gave this up a few years ago because it was getting in the way of the actual writing. She returned to fiction, which she much prefers, and there's a novel in progress.

Scene and staging

It should be possible to present this play either on a stage or in a classroom. There are three acting areas:

1 Front of stage – Vanessa's flat. It's indicated by a table and chair. She looks out of (imaginary) window at kids, policemen etc.

2 Back of stage – the street, the kids' area. It's divided from the front by a line of jackets and anoraks, laid down by the kids in scene 1 about quarter of the way downstage and moved forward by degrees in later scenes. Alex and Chris make sorties beyond the line, towards front stage. The other kids cross to and fro in a tentative or 'daring' way. Vanessa never crosses the line until the end of scene 11.

3 Prompt corner – used only for TV report, scene 12.

Some lighting effects are indicated, but if lighting is not possible, music/ sound effects can be substituted, for example, a clash of cymbals to equal blackout. Where lighting available, music etc. can of course still be used.

The setting is presented as Glasgow, but it can be anywhere – place names can be changed and local accents used. In whatever setting, there should be a clear distinction of accent between the 'front stage' characters and the kids.

Alex and Chris: These are written as a boy and a girl, but they could both be girls, or boys.

Optional characters: if not enough actors available, these characters can be offstage, spoken to or 'seen' by Vanessa.

Kids: as many as available. If necessary they can be a 'stage army', coming on and off to give illusion of numbers. Their functions are:

● to report offstage action, bring in plunder, etc. – no lines, or only improvised ones.

● to mutter, sing, jeer etc. as required – mostly improvised.

● to move the 'wall' of jackets forward as indicated in script.

SCENE ONE

*The stage is empty except for a table and chair at the front.
Enter VANESSA with FIONA and JAMIE (or without, see notes
on 'Optional characters') and JUDITH. VANESSA heads for
table and dumps shopping bags, schoolbags etc. on it.
JUDITH comes in tentatively, looking nervously behind her.*

VANESSA: *(Looking out of 'window' towards back of stage)* It's all right, they haven't arrived yet.

JUDITH: I shouldn't stay long.

VANESSA: Oh go on, a coffee, it's been ages.

JUDITH: I don't like to leave the house. Graffiti. You know. Next door had a window broken last week.

VANESSA: See, Judith, I keep telling you, tenements are a good idea. Two floors up? We're out of range.

JUDITH: You hope.

VANESSA: I'll just phone Mrs D. *(Does so, probably on mobile)* Hello, love, I picked up some milk for you, do you want to pop down?

FIONA: *(If she's there)* I'll take it up for you, Mummy.

VANESSA: *(If Fiona's not there, calling to her offstage)* No, that's all right, darling, Mrs Davidson will come down. You've got your homework to do.

JUDITH: I suppose you don't want her...

VANESSA: Out on the stair by herself. No, I'd rather not.

JUDITH: But you do have a security door.

VANESSA: *(Whispering, especially if children are there)* Easily kicked in.

Enter MRS DAVIDSON, elderly neighbour. Picks up milk.

MRS DAVIDSON: Thank you, Vanessa. That's very kind of you. They're not there yet.

VANESSA: No. It's early enough.

MRS DAVIDSON: I think they're arriving earlier than they used to.

VANESSA: Well, clocks forward, lighter evenings...

MRS DAVIDSON: Did you think there were more yesterday?

VANESSA: *(Glances at JUDITH, and children if they're there)* Maybe one or two extra.

MRS DAVIDSON: More than that. It used to be two or three. Then five or six. Yesterday there must have been eight or ten. There'll be more today, you mark my words.

At back of stage KIDS begin to enter by ones and twos. Lean against side of stage, chat idly, talk on mobiles, listen to iPods, etc.

VANESSA: *(To MRS DAVIDSON)* Well, you'd better get upstairs, you're all right for your cuppa now!

MRS DAVIDSON: I thought I might shut the storm door. I know it's early. Do you think I'm silly?

VANESSA: No, you do that.

Exit MRS DAVIDSON

JUDITH: *(Nervously)* I won't stay, Vanessa.

VANESSA: *(Sighs)* Well, if you're sure.

JUDITH: I really can't. They'll be there by now. You know, at the traffic lights. They press the button for the green man and then they don't cross.

VANESSA: They do that here too. *(Doubtfully)* Doesn't do any harm really. I suppose they've got nothing better to do.

JUDITH: We did mention it to the police, they came and moved them on.

VANESSA: But they just regroup, don't they. Along the road. At the next set of lights.

JUDITH: And they outnumber the police. Five to one, I'd say. At the very least.

VANESSA: I never thought of that.

JUDITH: *(Looking out of 'window')* I think they're coming now.

> *The KIDS are definitely moving in by now. Four or five of them take off jackets/anoraks and lay them across the stage in a line, about quarter way downstage – the symbolic line dividing 'front' – VANESSA – from 'back' – KIDS.*

VANESSA: Putting down their jackets. Goalposts maybe?

JUDITH: It's not football they're playing.

VANESSA: *(Looks for a minute, then turns away abruptly)* I'll see you out.

JUDITH: *(Looking back as she exits nervously)* They aren't very near.

> *Exit JUDITH and VANESSA, and children if they're there. Front of stage empty. At back of stage, more KIDS come in, hang about, sit down etc. – making themselves at home. We should notice ALEX and CHRIS near front of crowd, obviously together. ALEX steps over line of anoraks, holds out his hand to CHRIS, who jumps over. Blackout/clash of cymbals, as available.*

SCENE TWO

> *Lights up, or 'morning' music. Enter VANESSA, well towards front of stage, with bottle of milk, bag of rolls. The KIDS are lounging, some sleeping, but begin to wake as she comes in.*

VANESSA: *(Calling back over her shoulder as if to shopkeeper)* Thank you! Morning!

CHRIS: *(Imitating her upper-crust accent)* Thenk yeow! Mawnin!

KIDS: *(Perhaps mostly girls, the occasional boy in falsetto, the mocking phrases picked up around the group)* Mawnin! Thenk yeow! Mawnin! Oh I say! Jolly good show!

VANESSA stops for a moment, startled, then tosses her head and makes for her 'house'. ALEX emerges from crowd, deliberately steps over line of anoraks.

ALEX: *(Politely)* Morning.

VANESSA: *(It's a reflex response)* Morning. *(Annoyed with herself)* Excuse me, I'm really in a bit of a rush.

ALEX: *(Still polite)* Won't keep you then.

VANESSA: *(Staring at him)* What...Who...What are you kids doing here? Haven't you got anything better to do?

ALEX: *(Progressively more of the local accent from now on)* Whit would you like us to be daein?

VANESSA: What? Well...How should I know? Haven't you got school to go to?

ALEX: Dogged it *(Or local equivalent)* merr'n I was there an then I chucked it. *(Mimicking a headmaster, though still in his own accent)* No exactly uni material, Alexander, I think you'll agree.

VANESSA: Well. A job then?

ALEX: A job? Whit's that?

VANESSA: I'm sure you're not supposed to...gather...In numbers, like that...The police will move you on...

ALEX: They can try.

VANESSA stares at him for a minute, then flounces into the 'house', puts milk and rolls on table.

VANESSA: *(Calling to offstage children)* Fiona! Jamie! All right, darlings? Breakfast and then it's time for school!

Short blackout and/or hurry-scurry music. KIDS possibly drink from cans, eat sausage butties, etc. VANESSA clears away milk and rolls, comes back and sits down at table with phone.

SCENE THREE

Throughout this scene Vanessa is speaking on the phone and listening to replies.

VANESSA: Hello Judith? How are you, all right? No, okay here... I say though, it's really annoying, the takeaway seems to have closed...Yours too? Just too much hassle I suppose...And you, love. Take care.

VANESSA: Hello Margaret? Vanessa here. I know, it's been ages... No, Judith feels the same...Break-ins, yah, that sort of thing...No, nothing special...Yes, but they're not doing anything exactly, just kind of sitting there...Yah, speak to you soon.

VANESSA: Hello Tracy? Yes, it's Vanessa. Just thought I'd...What, last night? Oh, I'm sorry to hear that, love...No, won't keep you, I'll call in a day or two.

VANESSA: Hello Liz? No, no worse, not really. What's it like with you? Do you have...Yes, same here. Do they...Yes, same sort of thing. I don't suppose they're...No, not doing any harm, really...

During her conversation the KIDS are coming and going. ALEX is in the centre of the crowd, issuing orders etc. As she finishes, our attention is drawn to the group – a couple of girls start jumping back and forward over the line of anoraks, as if jumping rope. Two small boys run in with plunder (laptop? car tyre? baker's tray of rolls?) and show to ALEX. We hear him say 'aye, great, excellent', or current phrase of approval. A couple of boys pick up anoraks, look at ALEX for approval, move anoraks forward one by one, so that the line is now slightly farther downstage.

SCENE FOUR

Enter MRS DAVIDSON, carrying shopping, about half way downstage – still on 'front' side of anorak line. Small KIDS get in her way, jostle her, she stops in a fluster, drops one of her shopping-bags. ALEX sees this, snaps fingers at small kids.

ALEX: Come on youse, pick up the wumman's messages.

They do so and scuttle away. ALEX stands in front of her. CHRIS emerges from crowd and snuggles up to him.

MRS DAVIDSON: *(Nervously)* Thank you.

ALEX: You're welcome. On you go now, pit the feet up, get the kettle on. In the town all day, takes it oot o you.

MRS DAVIDSON: Oh, I wasn't…I just slipped out for a few minutes…

ALEX: Ten thirty-five you left and let's see *(Looks at watch)* that's four o'clock I make it now.

MRS DAVIDSON: You know…You were watching…

ALEX: Oh aye, Mrs Davidson. Did you no know that?

MRS DAVIDSON whimpers and tries to get past. ALEX steps politely aside, CHRIS takes her time.

CHRIS: You remind me o my gran. *(As MRS DAVIDSON smiles in relief)* Batty ould getherup. *(Or whatever's the current dismissive phrase for old ladies)*

MRS DAVIDSON: *(Bravely)* She wouldn't like to see you here!

CHRIS: Nae place else for me to go, hen.

MRS DAVIDSON: School? Job?

CHRIS: *(Shriek of laughter)* Job? Whit's that?

The KIDS behind her laugh, yell, catcall, as MRS DAVIDSON scuttles into VANESSA'S 'house'.

SCENE FIVE

MRS DAVIDSON bursts in on VANESSA, who's still at the table with her phone.

MRS DAVIDSON: Oh Vanessa...they stopped me...I couldn't get past...

VANESSA: Who? Not...

MRS DAVIDSON: Yes. Them. Two of them.

VANESSA: *(Taking shopping, sitting her down)* Oh, love, there, there, breathe deeply. What...what did they do?

MRS DAVIDSON: Well...nothing. They...they spoke to me.

VANESSA: What did they say?

MRS DAVIDSON: Nothing...really...I'm being silly. On the bus, coming home, Vanessa. It was so strange. The bus was late...

VANESSA: Well, that's situation normal.

MRS DAVIDSON: And everybody was so glad to get it. So relieved when it came. As if it was the last bus there was ever going to be.

VANESSA: *(Looks out of 'window')* I've thought for a day or two...I'm sure there aren't as many buses as usual.

MRS DAVIDSON: Even the drivers...Two or three...kids...jumped on ahead of me. Didn't pay. The driver didn't say a word. They sat down at the front, you know?

VANESSA: Elderly, disabled, infirm...

MRS DAVIDSON: People with sticks! Had to stand! Nobody dared to say a word! And one of the kids, he shouted across the bus 'Where are you today?' The other one said 'Snob Cross'. The first one, 'Me too.' As if they were...

VANESSA: Organised.

MRS DAVIDSON: And they got off here.

VANESSA: Yes. Snob Cross.

MRS DAVIDSON: *(Reprovingly)* Cobhill Cross. A very good address.

VANESSA: Snobhill Cross. That's what the bad boys called it in primary school. Snob Cross for short.

(Turning to face audience) Snob, terrible term of insult in Glasgow and district. Joke: Guidance teacher berating boy, calls him among other things a slob. Boy loses head, shouts will get faither up, nae right calling me a snob. Teacher, bemused: Wait a minute, I didn't say snob, I said slob. Boy: Oh, that's all right then.

(Still speaking to audience, or maybe to herself) But we're nice people here in Cobhill. We have mortgages. Good schools. Red sandstone tenements, tiled closes *(or other local shibboleths)*. You find us all over. West End, South Side. White-collar. Professional people. Middle-class. We're *nice* people. We *(She falters)*...we don't do any harm...not really.

MRS DAVIDSON: *(Behind her)* We could go away, Vanessa. Till it's all settled down.

VANESSA: *(Turning to her again)* Fiona and Jamie...their schoolwork...

MRS DAVIDSON: Away from here? A nice wee country town?

She could mention a couple of names here – most effective if they're towns superficially idyllic but locally known to have problems.

VANESSA: Leave our houses? They'd wreck our houses.

MRS DAVIDSON: What does that matter? Oh...*(Apologetically)* I forgot, you have a mortgage, dear.

VANESSA: Well...we might have to...*(Decisively)* Yes! Let's do that!

MRS DAVIDSON: Except...the thing is...

VANESSA: *(Impatiently)* What?

Murmuring and restlessness from the KIDS has become obvious again.

MRS DAVIDSON: Are we sure...they...aren't in the country towns too?

VANESSA: No. We're not sure of that.

They stand and look at one another for a moment.

VANESSA: I'll see you upstairs. And I'll check the close doors, front and back.

As VANESSA and MRS DAVIDSON exit, noise from the KIDS swells up. Running forward and back over the anorak line. Stray voices.

KIDS: Check the front. Check the back. Windaes, mind and check the windaes. Whit about the roof?

Culminating in blackout or cymbal crash.

SCENE SIX

Lights up, or 'busy' music as before. There are more KIDS in crowd – or they're coming and going to give that effect – and they're moving the line of anoraks forward until it's about half way downstage. Enter VANESSA with three or four shopping bags. She's breathing fast from panic as much as exertion. She enters about level with anorak line – sees it's been moved – gasps and scurries farther downstage. As she comes round the end of anorak line, ALEX steps over it and stands in front of her.

ALEX: Hard day at the supermarket, Vanessa?

VANESSA: How do you...*(Pulls herself together)* Please mind your manners. You wouldn't like it if I called you...

ALEX: Called me...? *(He waits for a moment)* Well, you canny, can you, Vanessa? You've forgot ma name. You think you dinnae know it. *(Posh accent)* Actually you don't think I've got a name.

VANESSA: No...I remember, I do remember...you said...

ALEX: *(Ignoring her, looking at shopping bags)* Hmm, you've been busy. Maxed oot yer credit card I reckon. Canned soup. Sardines. Long-life milk. Crispbread. Hey, you forgot the candles an the duct tape. Aw no, candles, there they are.

VANESSA: It's my usual shopping night.

ALEX: Two of everything an aw. Panic buying is whit we cry that, Vanessa, hen.

VANESSA: What if it is? It's you, it's your fault!

ALEX: *(Innocent)* Me?

VANESSA: Yes, you! You stand there...you sit there...and you...and you...

ALEX: *(Interested)* We whit?

VANESSA: You won't let us cross the street in peace.

ALEX: Have we ever stopped youse? No us. It's yersels, *(He gestures towards anorak line:)* You're feart to cross the street.

VANESSA: You watch us all the time.

ALEX: Well, see, we're interested in youse, Vanessa. We want to know how you got to be the way yiz are. Which is merr'n youse want to know about us.

VANESSA: The way we are?

ALEX: Uh-huh. Youse. *(Pause)* So let's see then. You're gonny wall yourself up in there, two up right?

VANESSA: How do you know...?

ALEX: You've kept the weans off the school for two days.

VANESSA: It's going to be closed tomorrow anyway. Till further notice.

ALEX: *(Pleased)* That right? Hey, we done something there, eh? An the buses...Your wee deli's getting a bit low on the croissants, don't know how long they'll stay open.

VANESSA: The delivery vans won't come any more...Same in Shawlands...Same in Bearsden.

Behind them in crowd two KIDS act it out.

KIDS: 'It's you, nobody will come because of you...' 'Whit did we dae?'

ALEX: So you'll sit up there with yer candles an yer long-life milk an you're hopin we'll go away. Well, dream on, Vanessa. We'll no. No in Shawlands. No in Bearsden. No in Snob Cross.

VANESSA: *(Panicky)* I've got to go.

ALEX: You'll eat yer sardines an burn yer candles an you'll look oot the windae an we'll still be here. An will I tell you something, Vanessa? You'll still not know our names.

VANESSA: Must go, must get in.

She's rummaging in her pockets.

ALEX: Lookin for yer key, Vanessa? You'll no need it. Somebody's kicked yer security door in. *(Posh accent)* Sorry I didn't quite catch his name.

Flashing lights, jangled music, KIDS muttering and moving to and fro. Puts her bags on the table at front. Enter MRS DAVIDSON, all of a fluster, to join her.

SCENE SEVEN

MRS DAVIDSON: The door...they've kicked the door in...heard them on the stairs.

VANESSA: *(Breathless)* Emergency arrangements...you take some of this, soup, candles...Look, we can rig up the old baby alarm, the mike in my flat and the speaker in yours...they'd get to me first...you'd hear.

MRS DAVIDSON: And what? What could I do?

VANESSA: Well...phone the police, yes, that's what to do.

MRS DAVIDSON: Do you think they'd come?

Two POLICEMEN can cross at extreme back of stage, but just as effective if VANESSA only 'sees' them – see notes on optional characters (page 152).

VANESSA: *(Looking out of 'window')* Oh look...there...two of them...in uniform...I didn't think they ever came here now.

MRS DAVIDSON: *(Also looking)* They're keeping a safe distance and no mistake. They're not looking anywhere near...

VANESSA: They've gone.

They stand looking for a moment or two. Noise from KIDS begins to rise with threatening effect.

MRS DAVIDSON: Well...I'd better...I can't leave the flat empty.

VANESSA: I'll see you in the morning.

SCENE EIGHT

Exit MRS DAVIDSON as VANESSA sits down at table. If FIONA and JAMIE are there, they creep in and she puts her arms round them, otherwise she buries her head in her arms. A night of anarchy is entirely conveyed by lights and/or sound effects – flashing light, discordant sound, KIDS rushing on and off, etc. Gradually it dies down, a few KIDS sit down, lie down, fall asleep. Lights up or morning music.

SCENE NINE

KIDS rouse at back of stage. Move unhurriedly forward, shift line of anoraks forward – it's nearly at the table now. VANESSA stirs, looks round nervously, creeps out on to what's left of front of stage. ALEX and CHRIS come forward to meet her.

ALEX: Bright an early out for the messages, Vanessa.

VANESSA: He might have some milk...maybe even eggs.

ALEX: A wee tip for you, hen. Get in plenty merr candles.

CHRIS: Ach, that was gonny be a surprise for her.

ALEX: Ach naw, I'm no like that. *(To VANESSA)* Naw, there's some guys doon at the sub-station. Should be able to dae something there. Pull a switch. Cut a cable.

CHRIS: Dangerous, mind you. High voltage.

ALEX: I've telt them tae wear their wellies, they'll be jake.
(Or current term for 'perfectly fine')

VANESSA: I hope they're not. I hope they kill themselves. *(Slowly, as she imagines the possibility)* I hope they burn to death. I hope they fry. *(Screaming)* I hope you all roast in hell!

ALEX: *(Mocking)* Aw, missis, that's no very nice of you.

A moment's silence – VANESSA has covered her face, is sobbing.

VANESSA: *(Brokenly)* What is it? What do you want?

CHRIS: We want you tae look at us.

VANESSA: What?

CHRIS: Look at us. That's a start anyway.

VANESSA raises her head and looks at them.

CHRIS: What dae you see?

VANESSA: I see...two...kids.

CHRIS: Who dae you see?

VANESSA: Two kids...I said.

CHRIS: Aye. Two kids. You pass us in the street an aw you see is two kids. *(Posh accent)* Oh, I say, that music's a bit on the loud side! Don't much care for your baseball cap, old boy!

VANESSA: That's not fair.

CHRIS: We haveny got names, have we? The kids, that's whit we are. Okay, listen up. I'm Chris. This is Alex. That's who we are.

VANESSA: But I still don't know you.

CHRIS: Naw. We're the kids. We couldny cope at school an we canny get jobs.

ALEX: An there youse are wi yer bought houses an yer kids at their posh schools.

CHRIS: An we've naethin to dae an naewhere to go.

VANESSA: *(Feebly)* It's not my fault.

ALEX: Whose is it then?

VANESSSA, sobbing, rushes into her 'house', flings herself down at table. ALEX and CHRIS link arms and saunter upstage.

CHRIS: *(Posh accent)* I say, Alexander, madam's in a little bit of a tizzy, what?

ALEX: *(Likewise)* I do believe you're right, Christina, old girl.

CHRIS: *(Her own voice)* Nane the wiser but.

ALEX: No a scooby.

Ideally, a flash or cymbal clash, with triumphant reaction from KIDS – the sub-station's blown up.

SCENE TEN

KIDS settle down. ALEX and CHRIS are among them. They're now sitting all over the stage, as far as the anorak line. The light is dim (no electricity). They're leaning against each other and singing quietly, maybe 'Kumbayah'. VANESSA is at table, stabbing numbers into her mobile, saying a few broken words, switching off. Enter MRS DAVIDSON.

MRS DAVIDSON: Are you all right, dear? It's quite quiet on the stair. They're all outside, they're just sitting there.

'Kumbayah' rises and falls throughout these speeches.

VANESSA: They're singing. They've won. They think they have. But they haven't. Mrs D, can you stay here for...oh...ten minutes? I want to be across the street by quarter to four.

MRS DAVIDSON: Across the street? But they're all there.

VANESSA: I know. But the policemen. They passed at the same time yesterday. I'm sure they'll be back today.

MRS DAVIDSON: *(Maundering)* You'd think they'd do something...I suppose it would be two against...

VANESSA: They will do something. I'll make them do something. I've got to get to the policemen, I'll tell them...

MRS DAVIDSON: You could call out to them, dear.

VANESSA: The singing would drown my voice.

And 'Kumbayah' swells now – the KIDS stir, get up, move around – ALEX stands up in the middle of the crowd.

SCENE ELEVEN

*Ominous music, flashing lights, etc. as VANESSA deliberately
moves out from behind the table and upstage. Cheers from
the KIDS. She crosses the anorak line for the first time. ALEX
blocks her way.*

ALEX: Come to see whit we're like? Who we are?

VANESSA: Get out of my way.

ALEX: Aw, Vanessa.

VANESSA: The policemen...I've got to get to them...There they
are...*(Upstage, either real or 'seen' by her, as before)*

ALEX: *(Mocking)* The sodgers? *(Or current dismissive term)* They're no
lookin at you, hen. They dinnae care. Dinnae even know
who you are. Same as you don't...

VANESSA: *(Screams)* Get out of my way!

*She flings herself at him, attacks him – KIDS join in – free-for-
all, flashing lights, cymbals, blackout.*

SCENE TWELVE

Takes place in prompt corner, if possible brightly lit while rest of stage is dark. TOBY BARKER with hand mike, KIDS milling about, MRS DAVIDSON shrinking at his side.

TOBY BARKER: This is Cobhill Cross in the west end of Glasgow, where earlier today a young man was taken to hospital with severe lacerations and suspected internal injuries. A woman who also sustained injuries in the incident is reported to be helping police with their enquiries. *(Reaction from KIDS during his speech, cheers, jeers, groans etc.)* The residents of this pleasant, er, residential district see today's incident as the climax of a campaign of harassment by young unemployed people. Mrs Davidson, you live here in Cobhill Road?

MRS DAVIDSON: I wish you wouldn't give...Well...Never mind.

TOBY BARKER: I believe you've had a lot of harassment from these young people?

MRS DAVIDSON: Well...yes...no...

KIDS: *(From crowd, sharing the phrases among two or three)* Hi there, Mrs Davidson ninety-five Cobhill Road...three up right.

TOBY BARKER: The young people themselves take a different view.

CHRIS: *(Emerging from crowd)* She went aff her head so she did. Pure mental so she is *(Or current expression for 'unbalanced')*. Comes oota her close an makes a dive at Alex. He tries to get oota the road. She goes for him, teeth, nails, decks him, he disnae want tae touch her, he canny get away.

MRS DAVIDSON: It wasn't like that at all! She was trying to speak to the police! That boy, he wouldn't let her past, it was the last straw.

KIDS chant, a wordless jeer, drowning her out – somebody starts up 'Kumbayah'.

MRS DAVIDSON: *(Shouting, in their general direction)* It's your fault. Your fault. *(To TOBY BARKER)* She'd never have...they've driven her mad...it was all because of them...

KIDS: *(From crowd, scattered, innocent, mocking voices)* Us?...Us?...Us?

TOBY BARKER: *(Hastily)* Toby Barker, News at Eighteen, Cobhill Cross.

> *Quick blackout, or cymbals clash.*

END OF PLAY

Activities

Report writing

You are going to write a news story for a website or a newspaper reporting on or analysing what happened at Cobhill Cross.

Using the play as your source, research your story. Your notes should include eye witness accounts, and details about who, where, when, what (happened), and why.

Study the layout and style of newspaper and website stories.

Write your story in a style that will appeal to the target audience and be appropriate for the publication.

Before you start writing think about:

- Which site/publication are you writing for?

- What is your purpose and angle?

- Who is your target audience?

- Where in the page/article will the report be placed?

- Is it a feature article or news report?

Summary of play

Write a brief summary of each scene.

Write a three sentence summary of the play which gets the following information across: who, context – where, when, social situation, and theme(s).

In a group, identify the three most important scenes and justify your choices. Give quotations to back up your choices.

Summary advice

Before you write a summary, list all significant information. Highlight three things you would need to tell someone if they were to have an idea of what the play is about.

Dramatic techniques

You are going to write 'mini-essays' about the dramatic techniques Moira Burgess has used to build tension in *The Snob Cross Incident*. These can be combined and linked to make a complete essay.

Write a mini-essay for each of three or more dramatic techniques used in *The Snob Cross Incident*. You can use the example lines of thought given below, adapt them, or make up your own.

Check your own essays and those of a partner. Each should:

- have a topic sentence.

- explain or analyse how a dramatic technique has been used.

- refer only to information relevant to the line of thought.

- give evidence from the text to back up points made.

- evaluate the success/impact of the technique.

Give two stars and a wish feedback – two positive comments and one suggestion for improvement.

Suggested lines of thought for mini-essays:

> The changing position of the line of Kids' jackets is used as a powerful visual symbol to show the audience how far the Kids have invaded the lives of the (Cobhill) Cross residents and build a sense that something bad is bound to happen.

> Conflict between Alex and Chris and Vanessa escalates each time they meet and adds to the impact of their final confrontation.

> Increasingly sinister sound effects and lighting contribute greatly to the tension throughout the play and give impact to the key incidents and the climax.

Suggested essay title:

> By (close) reference to a play you know well, show how dramatic techniques help build tension and contribute to the success of the climax.

If you are going to use the mini-essays in the complete essay, decide on the order and write links.

Discussion

VANESSA: *(Feebly)* It's not my fault.
ALEX: Whose is it then?

Whose fault is it then? Who or what causes the kind of social unrest seen in *The Snob Cross Incident*? Kids; the 'Snobs'; the government; the police? Is it everyone's responsibilty or no one's?

With others, discuss the reasons for the kind of conflict seen in *The Snob Cross Incident*. Refer to events in the play and in wider society.

Evaluate your performance using the assessment criteria for your course.

Diagram of Stage Directions

USR	**USC**	**USL**
CSR	**CS**	**CSL**
DSR	**DSC**	**DSL**

– audience –

USR upstage right   **USC** upstage centre   **USL** upstage left

CSR centrestage right   **CS** centrestage   **CSL** centrestage left

DSR downstage right   **DSC** downstage centre   **DSL** downstage left